Annual Survey 2017

US Government & Politics

Anthony J. Bennett

Philip Allan Updates
Market Place
Deddington
OX15 0SE

Orders
Bookpoint Ltd, 130 Milton Park, Abingdon, Oxfordshire, OX14 4SB
tel: 01235 827720
fax: 01235 400454
e-mail: uk.orders@bookpoint.co.uk
Lines are open 9.00 a.m.–5.00 p.m., Monday to Saturday, with a 24-hour message answering service. You can also order through the Philip Allan Updates website: www.philipallan.co.uk

© Philip Allan Updates 2007

ISBN 978-1-84489-647-9

All rights reserved; no part of this publication may be reproduced, stored in a retrieval system, or transmitted, in any other form or by any means, electronic, mechanical, photocopying, recording or otherwise without either the prior written permission of Philip Allan Updates or a licence permitting restricted copying in the United Kingdom issued by the Copyright Licensing Agency Ltd, 90 Tottenham Court Road, London W1T 4LP.

Printed by Raithby, Lawrence and Co Ltd, Leicester

Environmental information
The paper on which this title is printed is sourced from managed, sustainable forests.

Contents

Preface — iv

Chapter 1 The Alito appointment to the Supreme Court — 1
O'Connor announces her retirement ■ John Roberts nominated, then withdrawn ■ Harriet Miers nominated, then withdraws ■ Samuel Alito nominated ■ Liberal groups gear up to oppose Alito ■ Senate confirmation ■ What's wrong with the hearings? ■ The Senate votes ■ Conclusion

Chapter 2 The O'Connor legacy on the Supreme Court — 13
Noteworthy judgements ■ Kennedy now seen as 'swing' justice

Chapter 3 The Supreme Court, 2005–06 — 17
A new Supreme Court ■ The 2005–06 term ■ Court statistics ■ The Roberts Court

Chapter 4 Bush and Congress: the first 6 years — 25
Factors that affect presidential success in Congress ■ Measuring presidential success in Congress ■ Bush's key legislative victories ■ Bush's veto record

Chapter 5 The 2008 Presidential election — 33
Why 2008 looks like the Democrats' year ■ More changes in the nominating calendar ■ National Conventions ■ The would-be presidential candidates

Chapter 6 The red and blue debate revisited — 41
The 50–50 nation thesis ■ More shades of purple than red v blue ■ Four myths about red v blue ■ The significance of Bill Clinton and George W. Bush ■ Conclusions

Chapter 7 The 2006 mid-term congressional elections — 50
The primaries ■ The Senate results ■ The House results ■ The results overall ■ Who voted for whom, and why? ■ Why did the Democrats win? ■ Regime change on Capitol Hill ■ Likely effects

Who's who in American politics 2007 — 70

Preface

The year 2006 was something of a watershed in US politics. There was a new Supreme Court for the first time in 12 years and we saw the end of the 12-year Republican majority in the House of Representatives. We witnessed the first manoeuvrings for the 2008 presidential election. These events are analysed in this year's edition of the *US Government & Politics Annual Survey*.

At the start of 2006, Samuel Alito was confirmed by the Senate as an Associate Justice of the US Supreme Court — President Bush's second nomination in the space of just a few months. Therefore, the decisions of the Supreme Court had an added importance, as they provided the first insight into the judicial philosophy of Justice Alito. Initial indications are that he is more conservative than the person he replaced, Justice O'Connor, marking a rightward shift in the Court.

We also consider the debate about red and blue America. In a year in which nine so-called red (Republican) states — Florida, Missouri, Montana, Nebraska, New Mexico, North Dakota, Ohio, Virginia and West Virginia — elected Democrat senators, it is worth questioning whether America is as deeply divided politically as some commentators claim.

The mid-term elections brought Democrat majorities to both the House and the Senate. What will this mean for President Bush in 2007 and beyond? Will a Democrat-controlled Congress exercise its oversight functions more effectively than the Republicans managed? Will George W. Bush still be able to appoint conservative judges to the federal courts now that they have to be confirmed by a Democrat-controlled Senate? Will the President discover the usefulness of the veto power?

It will be interesting to observe how the new Democrat leadership in Congress shapes up. Will they implode, like the Republican's Newt Gingrich in the 1990s? Perhaps the Democrat old guard chairing the House and Senate standing committees will look tired and out of date — a kind of congressional equivalent of Bob Dole's 1996 presidential campaign.

2007 will be the starting gun for the 2008 presidential race. In what is the most open race for over 50 years, both parties have to make difficult decisions about their candidates. Will Democrat Hillary Clinton hold her position as front-runner and become the first woman presidential candidate of a major party? Will Republican John McCain hold his front-runner position and become the oldest presidential candidate of a major party in modern times?

These are the questions that we shall see answered during 2007. You will be answering other questions — those that you encounter in your examinations. I wish you all success and trust that this slim volume will help you in some way to secure the grades you are seeking.

Anthony J. Bennett, Charterhouse, Godalming, Surrey

Chapter 1
The Alito appointment to the Supreme Court

What you need to know
- The United States Supreme Court is made up of nine justices: one chief justice and eight associate justices.
- Nominations to the Court are made by the president, with the advice and consent of the Senate.
- Appointments to the Court are for life.
- For this reason, the president can make a nomination only upon the death or voluntary retirement of a member of the Court.
- On average, appointments are made approximately every 2 years.
- There were no vacancies on the Court between 1994 and 2005.

O'Connor announces her retirement

Four days after the end of the Court's 2004–05 term, associate justice Sandra Day O'Connor sent a simple, three sentence letter to President Bush. Dated 1 July 2005, the letter read:

> This is to inform you of my decision to retire from my position as an Associate Justice of the Supreme Court of the United States effective upon the nomination and confirmation of my successor. It has been a great privilege, indeed, to have served as a member of the Court for 24 terms. I will leave it with enormous respect for the integrity of the Court and its role under our Constitutional structure.

O'Connor was 75 and had served on the Court since her appointment by President Reagan in 1981. She was the first woman ever appointed to the Supreme Court. Her appointment had also been unusual in that she was recruited not from the federal appeal courts — the normal recruitment pool for Supreme Court justices — but from the Arizona state appeal court.

Appearing in the White House Rose Garden an hour after receiving the letter, President Bush praised O'Connor as 'a discerning and conscientious judge' and promised to nominate a successor 'who will faithfully interpret the Constitution'. The President added:

> The nation deserves and I will select a Supreme Court justice that Americans can be proud of. The nation also deserves a dignified process of confirmation in the United States Senate, characterised by fair treatment, a fair hearing and a fair vote.

These latter comments were oblique references to the standoff between the Republican President Bush and Senate Democrats over the Senate's treatment of a significant number of the President's lower federal court nominations in recent years. The President then phoned Justice O'Connor and they had what was described as an emotional conversation. Referring to O'Connor's Arizona background, the President joked: 'For an old ranching girl, you turned out pretty good!'

John Roberts nominated, then withdrawn

The announcement that the President was nominating Judge John Roberts to the Supreme Court came on 19 July, just 18 days after O'Connor's resignation letter. The initial reaction to the Roberts nomination was pleasing to the White House: Republicans rushed to praise him as a superb jurist, and even leading Democrats made comments that were not hostile to the nominee. The Senate Minority Leader, Harry Reid, noted that Roberts had 'suitable legal credentials' to be a member of the Supreme Court.

But then on 3 September 2005 the death was announced of Chief Justice William Rehnquist. In creating a second vacancy on the Supreme Court, Rehnquist's death threw the selection process for O'Connor's successor into disarray. If Rehnquist's seat was not filled by 3 October, the Court would begin its new term with only eight justices on the bench. O'Connor had already announced that she would remain on the Court until her successor was confirmed by the Senate. Therefore, President Bush decided on a switch of personnel. In a Labor Day press conference the White House announced that the President had withdrawn the nomination of John Roberts for the O'Connor vacancy and was now nominating him for the Rehnquist vacancy instead, hoping thereby to fill Rehnquist's seat by the beginning of the new term. The President would now have to find someone else to fill the O'Connor vacancy.

Harriet Miers nominated, then withdraws

With John Roberts now confirmed and sworn in as chief justice of the United States, President Bush made another nomination:

> In our great democracy, the Supreme Court is the guardian of our constitutional freedoms and the protector of our founding promise of equal justice under the law.
>
> Over the past five years I have spoken clearly to the American people about the qualities I look for in a Supreme Court justice. A justice must be a person of accomplishment and sound legal judgement. A justice must be a person of fairness and unparalleled integrity. And a justice must strictly apply the Constitution and the laws of the United States and not legislate from the bench.

This summer, I nominated an individual to the high court who embodies all these characteristics. And this morning, our nation can be proud when John Roberts opens a new Supreme Court session as the 17th chief justice of the United States.

It is now my duty to select a nominee to fill the seat that will be left vacant by the retirement of Justice Sandra Day O'Connor. This morning I am proud to announce that I am nominating Harriet Ellen Miers to serve as an associate justice of the Supreme Court.

Miers was an unusual nominee. First, she had no experience as a judge. As Table 1.1 shows, of the 109 Supreme Court justices nominated up to this point, 49 of them had been either a federal or state court judge. The last person to join the Supreme Court without such experience was William Rehnquist in 1971. Second, she was seen as a crony of the President. A fellow native of Texas, Miers had come to Washington in 2001 and had held a number of jobs in the Bush White House, rising to Counsel to the President in February 2005. Third, hardly anybody had heard of her. True, the President knew her. He said as much in announcing her nomination: 'I've known Harriet for more than a decade, I know her heart, I know her character.' But to most, it was a case of 'Harriet who?' Fourth, it transpired that the person who had promoted her name in the list of possible nominees was the *Democrat* leader in the Senate, Harry Reid of Nevada. President Bush was beset with significant domestic problems at the time, associated with what many saw as the federal government's inadequate response to the aftermath of Hurricane Katrina, which had hit the gulf coast states the previous month. It appeared as if Harriet Miers was the stealth candidate for the Supreme Court: unknown and therefore uncontroversial.

Jobs held previously	Most recent example (date)	Number of nominees holding this position
Federal judge	John Roberts (2005)	31
Practicing attorney	Lewis Powell (1971)	22
State court judge	Sandra Day O'Connor (1981)	18
Cabinet member	Arthur Goldberg, Labor Secretary (1962)	14
Senator	Harold Burton of Ohio (1945)	7
State governor	Earl Warren of California (1953)	3
Justice department official	William Rehnquist (1971)	3
Law professor	Felix Frankfurter (1939)	2
State legislator	Benjamin Curtis of Massachusetts (1851)	2
Solicitor General	Thurgood Marshall (1967)	2

Source: www.cq.com

Table 1.1 Jobs held by Supreme Court nominees at the time they were nominated, 1789–2004

Chapter 1

The initial reaction to the President's announcement was bafflement. Republicans were concerned that Miers too closely resembled Supreme Court justice David Souter, whom the President's father had put on the Court in 1990. Souter, virtually unknown at the time of his nomination, was said to be a conservative judge, but he has turned out to be one of the most liberal members of the Supreme Court. Democrats were puzzled. 'We know next to nothing about [Miers'] legal philosophy', said Senator John Kerry of Massachusetts. Meanwhile, William Kristol, editor of the influential conservative magazine *The Weekly Standard*, said he was 'disappointed, depressed and demoralised' by the President's nomination of Miers. It was not a promising start. In the *Washington Post*, columnist E. J. Dionne mused that for the President, choosing Miers 'risks looking like a sign of weakness'.

Within days of President Bush announcing the Miers nomination, conservative politicians and columnists were being vocally disparaging of the choice. 'Withdraw This Nominee' was the headline of Charles Krauthammer's syndicated column on 7 October:

> There are 1,084,504 lawyers in the United States. What distinguishes Harriet Miers from any of them, other than her connection with the President? By choosing a nominee suggested by Senate Democratic leader Harry Reid and well known only to himself, the President has ducked a fight on the most important domestic question dividing liberals from conservatives: the principles by which one should read and interpret the Constitution. For a presidency marked by a courageous willingness to think and do big things, this nomination is a sorry retreat into smallness.

Others weighed in against the Miers nomination, including former Bush speechwriter David Frum, former federal judge (and failed Supreme Court nominee) Robert Bork and conservative radio host Rush Limbaugh. Things went from bad to worse, for when Miers returned a completed questionnaire to Senate Judiciary Committee chairman Arlen Specter, the Republican senator said that her responses were inadequate and incomplete and he asked her to redo them.

On 27 October, just 24 days after being nominated, Miers wrote to the President:

> I write to withdraw as a nominee to serve as an Associate Justice of the Supreme Court of the United States. I am concerned that the confirmation process presents a burden for the White House and our staff and is not in the best interest of the country.

The President announced:

> Today I have reluctantly accepted Harriet Miers' decision to withdraw her nomination to the Supreme Court of the United States.

'This thing never got off the launch pad,' bemoaned a senior White House official. Miers was just too much of an unknown quantity, too inexperienced and too closely tied to President Bush.

> **Blame the right wing, or the concern about the concern?**
> **by Dana Milbank**
>
> Not two hours after the White House withdrew Harriet Miers' Supreme Court nomination yesterday morning, Senator Trent Lott (Republican–Mississippi) walked out of the Senate chamber with a spring in his step.
>
> 'I raised red flags the first day,' the Senator from I-told-you-so said. Asked if there was a sense of relief amongst Republicans, Lott paused, smiled and, in his barbershop-quartet bass sang out to disbelieving reporters: 'Happy Days Are Here Again!'
>
> Senators came to bury Miers yesterday, not to praise her. Republicans blamed the withdrawal on demands for White House documents. Democrats blamed right-wing ideologues. But few seemed distraught that the nation had been spared the equivalent of a televised bar exam before the Senate Judiciary Committee next month.
>
> 'It wasn't only the documents,' Miers' White House-assigned shepherd, former senator Dan Coats of Indiana, told reporters outside the Senate chamber. There was the prospect of a week of grilling by the Senate Judiciary Committee. 'She was,' Coats added, 'doing very well in her trial preparations.'
>
> Trial?
>
> 'Freudian slip,' the shepherd explained.
>
> Republican Senator Jeff Sessions of Alabama was not too distraught. 'I was concerned about the, uh, concern,' he said. 'Probably she was worried about it too.' Democrats, though never committed to supporting Miers, lined up to blame the 'right wing' (John Kerry), 'the far right wing' (Byron Dorgan), the 'extreme right wing' (Dick Durbin), 'extreme partisan pressure' (Mary Landrieu), and 'extremists' (Ted Kennedy).
>
> Source: **www.washingtonpost.com**, 28 October 2005

As shown in Table 1.2, President George W. Bush thus joined 14 other presidents who had suffered the ignominy of having a Supreme Court nomination either withdrawn or rejected (see Table 1.3). The *Washington Post* summed up the situation thus:

> President Bush's nomination of Harriet Miers was made from a position of weakness by a White House beset by political problems and eager to avoid a fight over the Supreme Court. Twenty-four excruciating days later, the supposed safe choice crashed, exposing the President as even weaker than before. It was an episode that seemed wholly out of character with the President's style. No Republican president has catered to the right more methodically than Bush. But on a matter of first-order significance to many conservatives, the President let personal loyalty override what had been a central tenet of his political strategy.

President	Dates	Number of Supreme Court nominees withdrawn	Number of Supreme Court nominees rejected
George Washington	1789–97	0	1
James Madison	1809–17	0	1
John Quincy Adams	1825–29	1	0
John Tyler	1841–45	3	1
James Polk	1845–49	0	1
Millard Fillmore	1850–53	3	0
James Buchanan	1857–61	0	1
Andrew Johnson	1865–69	1	0
Ulysses Grant	1869–77	2	1
Grover Cleveland	1893–97	0	2
Herbert Hoover	1929–33	0	1
Lyndon Johnson	1963–69	2	0
Richard Nixon	1969–74	0	2
Ronald Reagan	1981–89	1	1
George W. Bush	2001–	1	0

Source: *CQ Weekly*, 31 October 2005, p. 2908

Table 1.2 Supreme Court nominations withdrawn and rejected, 1789–2005

Justice	Date rejected	Nominated by
John Rutledge	1795	George Washington
Alexander Wolcott	1811	James Madison
John Spencer	1844	John Tyler
George Woodward	1845	James Polk
Jeremiah Black	1861	James Buchanan
Ebenezer Hoar	1870	Ulysses Grant
William Hornblower	1894	Grover Cleveland
Wheeler Peckham	1894	Grover Cleveland
John Parker	1930	Herbert Hoover
Clement Haynesworth	1969	Richard Nixon
Harrold Carswell	1970	Richard Nixon
Robert Bork	1987	Ronald Reagan

Table 1.3 Supreme Court nominees rejected by the Senate

This episode was one of the biggest political miscalculations of Bush's presidency — the failure to anticipate the opposition that the Miers nomination would provoke from his conservative base. The President's approval rating slumped below 40% for the first time in 5 years.

Samuel Alito nominated

It took the Bush White House just 4 days to come up with their third nominee for the O'Connor vacancy — Judge Samuel Alito. Having had no Supreme Court nominations for 11 years, this was now the fourth in just over 100 days (see Table 1.4). In choosing a federal judge of many years' standing and of sound conservative credentials, President Bush seemed to be saying to his conservative base, 'I hear what you're saying'. For in selecting what to many looked like a solid conservative judge to replace O'Connor (who had been seen as a 'swing' judge), Bush was potentially making a far greater impact on the Court than when he replaced conservative Chief Justice Rehnquist with Chief Justice Roberts. Steven Shapiro, national legal director of the American Civil Liberties Union (ACLU), a powerful liberal interest group, commented: 'Judge Alito's nomination calls into question the Court's delicate balance that Justice O'Connor has helped to shape and preserve.'

Date	Supreme Court nomination
19 July	John Roberts as associate justice
5 September	John Roberts as chief justice
3 October	Harriet Miers as associate justice
31 October	Samuel Alito as associate justice

Table 1.4 **President Bush's Supreme Court nominations, 2005**

Alito was born in Trenton, New Jersey in 1950, the son of an Italian immigrant. He graduated from Princeton (1971) and Yale Law School (1975). In 1990, the first President Bush nominated Alito to the US Appeals Court, and he received a unanimous backing in the Senate. Alito was about to become the second Italian-American on the Supreme Court (joining Antonin Scalia) and its fifth Roman Catholic. It would also leave the Court with only one woman for the first time since 1993.

The reaction of most Republicans ranged from pleased to thrilled. Democrats were disappointed, fearing that yet again — as with John Roberts — the President might have come up with a 'nice' conservative judge, about whom it would be difficult to rouse its own base into strident opposition. Alito might have the same views as fellow Italian Scalia, but he seemed to be able to express them in a less alarming fashion. He was no bull in a china shop. But liberal groups, such as ACLU, the AFL-CIO, NARAL, Pro-Choice America and MoveOn.org, all came out against Alito. That merely confirmed conservative Republicans in the belief that they were onto a good thing.

Liberal groups gear up to oppose Alito

In the weeks leading up to the Senate confirmation hearings, liberal pressure groups were organising their campaign to oppose the Alito nomination. The basis of their opposition was that while the earlier nomination of John Roberts to replace William Rehnquist was basically the nomination of one conservative judge to oppose another, there was evidence that Samuel Alito was more

conservative than Sandra Day O'Connor, and therefore this nomination, if successful, would mark a rightward swing for the Supreme Court.

Opponents were heartened by the fact that many senators remained undecided about Alito. 'Momentum is building in opposition,' claimed Nan Aron of the Alliance for Justice, one of the many liberal groups opposing Alito. Another group was IndependentCourt.org, a coalition of liberal groups who were seeking to build opposition through their website.

Senate confirmation

The hearings on the nomination of Judge Samuel Alito to the United States Supreme Court started on Monday 9 January 2006 and lasted 5 days, following a similar pattern to the Roberts hearings the previous September.

Day 1 began with 10-minute opening remarks from each of the members of the Senate Judiciary Committee — ten Republicans and eight Democrats — in order of seniority. Alito sat impassively until just before 3.30 p.m., when he was invited to deliver his opening statement. Without managing to summon up quite the eloquence and sparkle of John Roberts, Samuel Alito sought to send out the message that he is not an ideologue. Alito claimed that 'good judges are always open to the possibility of changing their minds', and that 'a judge can't have any agenda', nor have 'any preferred outcome in any particular case'.

Committee Democrats were not impressed, believing that Alito was purveying the same platitudes that they had heard just a few weeks earlier from John Roberts. To them, Alito was a conservative judge in disguise. Committee Republicans talked up Alito's impressive academic qualifications, his years of experience and what they regarded as his impressive rulings in lower courts. But Alito's previous rulings on such issues as abortion and the power of the presidency would mean that he would face a far more partisan Senate than had John Roberts.

On day 2, senators began their questioning of the nominee. Again, Alito sought to reassure on topical concerns. 'The Bill of Rights applies at all times,' he told the committee, adding that this was especially important at times of national crisis. Later he assured senators that he would approach the issue of abortion 'with an open mind'. And when asked about the current concern over warrantless eavesdropping by the Bush administration, Alito remarked that no one is 'above the law'.

According to *Washington Post* reporters Charles Babbington and Jo Becker, 'most of the committee's ten Republicans lobbed soft questions' at Alito, with the exception of Chairman Arlen Specter who, unlike most Republicans, supports abortion rights. He asked Alito about a memo the judge had written in 1985, in which he had stated that 'the Constitution does not protect a right to an abortion' — a clear repudiation of the Court's landmark 1973 *Roe* v

Wade decision. Alito explained this away by saying that this was what he thought at that time. When asked repeatedly whether it was still his view, Alito declined to answer.

But as the questioning continued, it became clear that even the Democrats did not have the stomach for a real fight over Alito. They had neither the public backing nor the votes to defeat him, and their questioning was long-winded and lacklustre. 'It was beginning to look as if the Democrats had shown up to a knife fight without a knife', commented the *Washington Post*. 'Dems fumble, Alito scores' was how the *New York Daily News* summed it up at the end of day 2, while to political commentator Robert Novak it looked like the Democrats were 'Shooting Blanks at Alito'. Democrat Joe Biden rambled on for 11 minutes before getting to his first question. Fellow Democrat Ted Kennedy threatened to disrupt the committee hearings if he wasn't given sight of some of Alito's private papers.

Things did not improve on day 3 as Alito's wife fled the room in tears following suggestions that her husband was a 'closet bigot'. Democrats focused on Alito's possible membership of a right-wing group, Concerned Alumni of Princeton, in the early 1970s. It seemed dimly relevant to most observers of the confirmation process and suggested that Democrats were thin on ammunition.

What's wrong with the hearings?

The Alito confirmation hearings didn't do as much harm to Judge Alito as it did to the senators themselves. Indeed, the episode merely added to widespread concern over the effectiveness of this check that the Senate has over presidential appointments. Ever since the furore over the Senate's rejection of Robert Bork as an associate justice of the Supreme Court in 1987, there have been concerns about the way the Senate conducts itself on such occasions. There would appear to be three distinct problems:

1 Senators from the president's party tend to use the occasion to throw soft questions at the nominee, not really trying to probe them for answers that might reveal whether or not they are suitably qualified for the job. This means that, provided a president has party control of the Senate, he can just about get anyone he wants confirmed by the Senate. That is not a recipe for effective checks and balances.
2 Senators from the opposition party tend to look for opportunities to attack and embarrass the nominee. They are often more interested in scandal, innuendo and gossip than in competence. This happened in the Clarence Thomas hearings in 1991 and, to a lesser extent, in the Alito hearings in 2006. Lacking civility and respect, the process has often teetered on the brink of the political equivalent of the WWF fights that are so popular on American television. Thomas Sowell had this to say in a piece he wrote on the Real Clear Politics website (**www.realclearpolitics.com**):

None of these ploys had anything to do with determining Judge Alito's qualifications to be on the Supreme Court. At most there were attempts to provoke him to anger with insulting questions in the hope of providing an excuse for Democrats to vote against him and for the weaker Republicans to be afraid to support him.

3 The confirmation process has become hugely partisan and often resembles a political campaign, with significant involvement of interest groups both in support of and opposed to the nominee. This is a relatively recent phenomenon. Just 20 years ago in 1986, Antonin Scalia — clearly a strict constructionist, conservative judge — was confirmed by the Senate without a single dissenting vote. It seems almost impossible to imagine that occurring today.

A few years ago, Calvin Mackenzie published a book with the title *Innocent Until Nominated: The Breakdown of the Presidential Appointment Process* (Brookings Institution Press, 2001). His conclusion was that the confirmation process is characterised by 'invasive scrutiny' and 'cruel and punishing publicity' for the nominee, which discourages qualified people from being prepared to be nominated for high office and thereby 'hinders the president's ability to govern'.

In January 2006 an editorial in the *Washington Post* — a liberal newspaper — described Alito as 'superbly qualified'. The editorial was headed simply 'Confirm Samuel Alito'. The editor wrote:

> Supreme Court nominations have never been free of politics, but neither has their history generally been one of party-line votes or of ideology as the determining factor. To go down that road is to believe that there is a Democrat law and a Republican law, which is repugnant to the ideal of the rule of law…No president should be denied the prerogative of putting a person as qualified as Judge Alito on the Supreme Court.

The *Washington Post* reported that over the 3-month period of the Alito nomination debate, 'hundreds of advocacy groups on both sides of the battle aggressively competed to shape public opinion, spending more than $2 million in advertising and blanketing the country with millions of e-mails'.

Yet not a single Democrat on the Senate Judiciary Committee voted to recommend the confirmation of Judge Alito. When the committee finally voted on 24 January, the vote was 10–8 — a strict party line vote.

The Senate votes

Now that the Senate Judiciary Committee had completed its work, the action moved to the Senate chamber. It was at this stage that Senate Democrats fell out among themselves as to whether to try to mount a filibuster on the Senate floor against the Alito nomination. The filibuster's leading supporters were the Massachusetts duo of Ted Kennedy and John Kerry. 'Judge Alito will take America backward, especially when it comes to civil rights and discrimination laws', stated John Kerry. Kennedy claimed that Alito 'does not share the values of equality and justice that make this country strong' and therefore 'does not deserve a place on the highest court of the land'. Encouraging them from the sidelines — and the television screens — were liberal interest groups such as People for the American Way and the NAACP as well as liberal web logs. But the Democrat leader in the Senate, Harry Reid of Nevada, made it clear that he did not support a filibuster on Alito. 'There has been adequate time for people to debate,' stated Reid, adding that he hoped 'this matter will be resolved without too much more talking.' The filibuster attempt turned out to be an embarrassing flop. Sixty votes are required to end a filibuster. When the vote came on 30 January, the vote was 72–25, with 19 of the 43 Democrats voting in favour of ending it.

The Senate immediately moved to a vote on the Alito nomination itself. Alito was confirmed by 58 votes to 42. All bar one Republican voted 'yes' and all bar four Democrats voted 'no'. The one Republican voting 'no' was Lincoln Chafee of Rhode Island, a liberal north-easterner who was up for re-election later in the year. The four Democrats supporting the Alito nomination were Ben Nelson of Nebraska, Kent Conrad of North Dakota, Tim Johnson of South Dakota and Robert Byrd of West Virginia. All four represent states won by George W. Bush in 2004 — so-called Red States. Three of the four (all bar Johnson) were up for re-election the same year.

Conclusion

It took George W. Bush almost 7 months to fill the Sandra Day O'Connor vacancy on the Supreme Court. Samuel Alito was the third person to be nominated. The nomination of John Roberts was withdrawn when the President nominated him for the William Rehnquist vacancy instead. The nomination of Harriet Miers was also withdrawn. According to Terry Eastland in the *Weekly Standard*, 'the big lesson from the search for O'Connor's successor is that quality matters'. Alito exhibited that quality and was duly confirmed.

The nomination also shows the importance for a president of having his party in the majority in the Senate. President Bush was able to secure the confirmation of his nominee because his own party — the majority party — had the votes it required. Democrats, meanwhile, failed to convince the country that nominees to the Supreme Court must be ideological mirror images of the justices they replace. Alito appears to be more conservative than O'Connor, yet he was still confirmed.

On 31 January 2006 Alito was sworn in as the nation's 110th Supreme Court justice. 'Sam Alito is a brilliant and fair-minded judge who strictly interprets the Constitution and laws and does not legislate from the bench,' said the President at the swearing-in ceremony. Bush clearly thinks he knows the mind of the judge he has chosen. But then his father thought he knew David Souter's mind when he put him on the Court in 1990. He was proved mistaken. We shall need to watch with interest the judgements that Samuel Alito makes on the Supreme Court in order to decide whether George W. Bush got this one right.

Chapter 2
The O'Connor legacy on the Supreme Court

During her 24 years on the Court, Sandra Day O'Connor gained a reputation as a pragmatic conservative. In the last 11 years, she often cast the deciding fifth vote as four conservative justices (Rehnquist, Scalia, Thomas and Kennedy) faced four liberal justices (Stevens, Souter, Ginsburg and Breyer). The hallmark of her style on the Court was described by law professor Cass Sunstein as 'judicial minimalism'. According to Professor Sunstein, O'Connor had been an implicit follower of the philosopher Edmund Burke, 'someone who likes tradition, respects incremental change and doesn't like revolution'. She would decide on each case separately, making a judgement that was no more far reaching than was absolutely necessary to deal with the particular problem highlighted. Not for her the grand sweeping judgements of *Brown* v *Board of Education of Topeka* (1954) or of *Roe* v *Wade* (1973). She always believed in keeping her options open for future cases.

But O'Connor was never in the solid conservative mould of colleagues Rehnquist, Scalia or Thomas. She tended to vote for conservative positions on crime, economic regulation and states' rights. But on abortion and race she was more liberal and pragmatic. E. J. Dionne, writing in the *Washington Post* the day after her resignation announcement, described her as a 'practical voice for partisan times'.

In her final terms on the Court she was reliably the justice who delivered the most majority opinions, and she therefore might be regarded as the justice most in tune with the mood of the nation. It was almost as if during the 1990s and into the current decade it was not so much 'the Rehnquist Court' as 'the O'Connor Court'.

Noteworthy judgements

Having served on the Court for so long, Justice O'Connor had participated in a large number of landmark decisions, and it is interesting to observe in how many of these decisions Justice O'Connor found herself in the majority. Table 2.1 shows 11 landmark decisions in which Justice O'Connor participated, covering a wide range of important issues, including flag desecration, abortion, gun control, campaign finance, capital punishment and affirmative action. In nine of these 11 landmark decisions, O'Connor found herself in the majority opinion, and six of those eight cases were decided by a 5–4 division of the Court.

Annual Survey, 2007

Chapter 2

Case	Concerning	Decision	O'Connor's position
Texas v Johnson (1989)	Texas state law forbidding flag burning declared unconstitutional	5–4	Minority
Planned Parenthood of SE Pennsylvania v Casey (1992)	Upheld Pennsylvania's limits on abortion rights	5–4	Majority
United States v Lopez (1995)	Gun-Free School Zones Act declared unconstitutional	5–4	Majority
Reno v ACLU (1997)	Communications Decency Act declared unconstitutional	7–2	Minority
Bush v Gore (2000)	Stopped Florida recount in 2000 presidential election	5–4	Majority
Ashcroft v Free Speech Coalition (2002)	Child Pornography Protection Act declared unconstitutional	7–2	Majority
Zelman v Simmons-Harris (2002)	Upheld Ohio school voucher programme	5–4	Majority
Atkins v Virginia (2002)	Execution of the mentally retarded declared unconstitutional	6–3	Majority
Gratz v Bollinger (2003)	University of Michigan undergraduate admissions affirmative action programme declared unconstitutional	6–3	Majority
Grutter v Bollinger (2003)	Upheld University of Michigan law school admission affirmative action programme	5–4	Majority
McConnell v FEC (2004)	Upheld Bipartisan Campaign Reform Act	5–4	Majority

Table 2.1 O'Connor's decisions in selected landmark cases, 1989–2004

Back in 1989, O'Connor dissented when the Court ruled (*Texas* v *Johnson*) that flag burning was a right protected by the 1st Amendment. Three years later, she concurred with the Court's 5–4 ruling in *Planned Parenthood of Southeastern Pennsylvania* v *Casey*, which in effect upheld the principle of a woman's right to an abortion, as announced in *Roe* v *Wade* (1973). In 1995, she was again in the majority of a 5–4 decision that declared the Gun-Free School Zones Act unconstitutional. In two decisions on pornography, Justice O'Connor came down on different sides of the argument, showing herself to be someone who was more of a pragmatist than an ideologue. In 1997 she was one of only two dissenters in *Reno* v *ACLU*, which declared the Communications Decency Act unconstitutional. Five years later, however, she was in the majority in *Ashcroft* v *Free Speech Coalition*, which struck down the Child Pornography Protection Act.

In 2000, O'Connor voted with the 5–4 majority that effectively made George W. Bush the 43rd president of the United States by putting a stop to any further recount of votes in Florida. In 2002, she was again in the majority in the 5–4 decision for *Zelman* v *Simmons-Harris*, which upheld the Ohio school voucher programme, thereby giving the majority to the conservative quartet of Rehnquist, Scalia, Thomas and Kennedy. In the same year she was again in the majority in *Atkins* v *Virginia*, by which the Court declared the execution of the mentally retarded to be unconstitutional.

O'Connor made decisive rulings on affirmative action programmes in the 2003 cases of *Gratz* v *Bollinger* and *Grutter* v *Bollinger*. Later the same year, with liberal justice John Paul Stevens, she co-authored the decision in *McConnell* v *Federal Election Commission*, which upheld the McCain-Feingold campaign finance law.

The fact that O'Connor had so often played the role of the 'swing justice' on the Court made President Bush's job of nominating a replacement even more critical. If it had been Chief Justice Rehnquist who had retired, Bush might have merely replaced one reliable conservative with another. But if Bush replaced O'Connor with a strictly conservative judge it might correctly be thought that he had moved the Court further to the right.

Kennedy now seen as 'swing' justice

The post-Sandra Day O'Connor Supreme Court seems to position Justice Anthony Kennedy at its centre as the 'swing' justice, the position previously held by O'Connor. To Kennedy's right are Chief Justice Roberts and associate justices Antonin Scalia, Clarence Thomas and, we presume, Samuel Alito. To his left are John Paul Stevens, David Souter, Ruth Bader Ginsburg and Stephen Breyer.

Take the issue of the death penalty — an area in which the Supreme Court has recently been called upon to make a number of judgements. In the 2002 landmark decision of *Atkins* v *Virginia*, the Court decided by a margin of 6–3 that executing mentally retarded people was unconstitutional, being a violation of the 8th Amendment right of freedom from 'cruel and unusual punishment'. In this decision, the four more liberal members of the Court — Stevens, Souter, Ginsburg and Breyer — were joined by 'swing justices' O'Connor and Kennedy to give the liberals the majority voice. Keith Perine commented in *CQ Weekly* (8 August 2005) that it was a decision of the 'O'Kennedy Court', as the Supreme Court has often been called. But with O'Connor gone and Roberts more likely to side regularly with the Court's conservative wing, Kennedy will be left to decide which group of four justices — the conservative or liberal group — he will join, thus turning one group into a majority of five.

Table 2.2 The likely ideological spectrum of the Supreme Court

Table 2.2 suggests how the new Supreme Court may line up ideologically — from Stevens on the left to Scalia on the right. Georgetown University law professor Mark Tushnet believes that the dynamic of the new Supreme Court may become 'a struggle for the soul of Anthony Kennedy conducted by John Roberts on his right and Stephen Breyer on his left'.

Of course, it is possible that Roberts or Alito could surprise us all and turn out to be different jurists from what first impressions might suggest. And that would not be that unusual. Three current members — Stevens, Kennedy and Souter — have all turned out to be rather different from initial expectations. All three jurists were appointed by Republican presidents — Gerald Ford, Ronald Reagan and George Bush respectively — but all have proven to be more liberal than expected. Picking Supreme Court justices can be rather like trying to pick the winner of the Grand National: you can study all the previous form, but in the end there may be an upset just around the corner.

Chapter 3

The Supreme Court, 2005–06

What you need to know
- The Supreme Court is the highest federal court in the USA.
- Supreme Court justices are appointed by the president and confirmed by the Senate.
- They are appointed for life.
- There are nine justices on the Supreme Court: one chief justice and eight associate justices.
- Of the current nine justices, seven have been appointed by Republican presidents and only two by Democrats.
- The Supreme Court has the power of judicial review. This is the power to declare acts of Congress or actions of the executive branch — or acts or actions of state governments — unconstitutional, and thereby null and void.
- By this power of judicial review, the Court acts as the umpire of the Constitution and plays a leading role in safeguarding Americans' rights and liberties.

A new Supreme Court

For the first time since 1994, the Supreme Court began its new term with a new justice, Chief Justice John Roberts. This was also the first change of chief justice for 20 years. During the term, the membership changed again. Four months into the Court's 2005–06 term, Sandra Day O'Connor finally stepped down with the confirmation of Samuel Alito. We have already considered these events, so this chapter will concentrate exclusively on the most important of the judgements handed down by the Supreme Court during this term.

The 2005–06 term

Perhaps because the membership of the Court had just changed, and because the new chief justice's intentions were for the Court to be less combative, the 2005–06 term did not go down as one of landmark proportions. That said, the term was dominated by one decision that may have profound effects on the understanding of presidential power in post-9/11 America. We shall consider four of the most significant judgements of the term as shown in Table 3.1.

Case	Concerning	Decision
Randall v Sorrell	Campaign finance	6–3
Hudson v Michigan	Search powers	5–4
Kansas v Marsh	Death penalty	5–4
Hamdan v Rumsfeld	Presidential power	5–3

Table 3.1 Significant Supreme Court decisions, 2005–06 term

Campaign finance

In the case of *Randall* v *Sorrell*, the Supreme Court declared unconstitutional a campaign finance law of the state of Vermont. The state legislature there had passed the law in 1997 in an attempt to tighten up the rules on what individuals and parties could give to election campaigns and also on what the candidates could spend. The limits were the toughest of any of the 50 states and were a direct challenge to the Supreme Court's 1976 ruling (*Buckley* v *Valeo*), which had been widely interpreted as saying that although contributions could be limited in order to stop corruption, limits on candidates' spending constituted an infringement of freedom of speech as guaranteed by the 1st Amendment. They had been signed into law in 1997 by the then state Governor, Howard Dean — now Chairman for the Democratic National Committee and a Democrat presidential candidate back in 2004.

> **Extract from 1st Amendment (1791)**
>
> 'Congress shall make no law...abridging the freedom of speech.'

In this 2006 decision, the Supreme Court again ruled against spending limits for candidates but allowed restrictions on contributions. However, for the first time, the Court ruled that specific limits that were set very low would not find favour with the Court. The Vermont law had limited contributions to as little as $200 per election for state-wide races.

The decision was reached by 6 votes to 3. The three dissenting justices were the three most liberal members of the Court — Souter, Stevens and Ginsburg. The majority opinion, authored by Stephen Breyer, stated two principles. First, it reiterated that any limits on the amount candidates may spend on their campaigns violate freedom of speech. Second, they ruled that although some limits on contributions would be allowed, those set by the Vermont law were far too low, thus potentially skewing political competition. There were indications that three justices — Kennedy, Scalia and Thomas — would have liked the Court to have gone further. Although they signed up to the majority opinion with Breyer, Roberts and Alito, they argued that they also opposed limits on campaign contributions as being against freedom of speech.

Search powers

In *Hudson* v *Michigan*, the Supreme Court ruled by five votes to four that the Constitution does not require that evidence gained through what are called 'no knock' searches must be excluded from the courtroom. This was an important ruling as the Court significantly changed its interpretation of the 4th Amendment right to protect citizens from 'unreasonable searches'. The case was brought by Booker T. Hudson, a Michigan man who was convicted of drug possession after police found crack cocaine in his pockets during a 'no knock' raid on his house in 1998.

In recent decades the Court had consistently ruled that evidence gathered improperly should be excluded from courtrooms. This so-called 'exclusionary rule' had been seen as a way of the Court protecting citizens' 4th Amendment rights. Some saw this as the first sign of the rightward shift of the Court following the replacement of Sandra Day O'Connor by Samuel Alito. A number of commentators suggested that O'Connor would have disagreed with this decision, thereby swinging the decision 5–4 in the other direction. The dissenting justices were the four most liberal members — Souter, Stevens, Ginsburg and Breyer.

Extract from 4th Amendment (1791)

'The right of the people to be secure in their persons, houses, papers and effects, against unreasonable searches and seizures, shall not be violated.'

At the heart of the decision was the so-called 'knock and announce' rule. This states that police searching a property must knock on the door and announce their arrival before entering. Back in 1995, in *Wilson* v *Arkansas*, the Court unanimously agreed that the 4th Amendment's protection against unreasonable searches included the common law principle of 'knock and announce'. Thus for the past 10 years, police officers carrying out a search had to presume that if they did not 'knock and announce' — and wait a reasonable time for a response before forcing their way in — they might lose any subsequent court case. But as a result of this 2006 case, the most they would have to fear would be an internal disciplinary case or a lawsuit for damages.

The 2006 case must also be seen against the backdrop of post-9/11 America and the so-called 'war on terror'. Civil liberties are often a casualty in time of war. In writing the majority opinion, Antonin Scalia focused on the number of guilty defendants who walk free from court because of evidence that has to be disregarded due to it being gained as a result of a 'no knock' search. He argued that American society and law enforcement had changed significantly since the Court had first announced the 'exclusionary rule' in 1961 (*Mapp* v *Ohio*), and he claimed that today's police forces are far more professional and careful about citizens' constitutional rights. Therefore he announced that the exclusionary rule was no longer necessary to enforce police compliance and that administrative and disciplinary procedures are now sufficient to safeguard citizens from unreasonable searches.

That line of reasoning brought a 30-page dissenting opinion from Justice Stephen Breyer. He failed to share Scalia's optimistic view of modern policing.

He concluded: 'Today's opinion weakens, perhaps destroys, much of the practical value of the Constitution's knock-and-announce protection.' In January 2006, when the justices first heard the case and cast tentative votes, O'Connor was still on the Court and her comments suggested she favoured Breyer's opinion rather than Scalia's. However, after she left at the end of that month, the Court announced it would hear the case again, an indication that without O'Connor's vote, the Court was in a 4–4 tie.

Death penalty

In yet another 5–4 decision, the Supreme Court upheld the death penalty in the state of Kansas. At first glance, the case of *Kansas* v *Marsh* was merely concerned with the constitutionality of Kansas's death penalty, which was reinstated after 22 years in 1994. The Kansas State Supreme Court had declared the state law unconstitutional, because it required jurors to impose the death penalty in cases where they found that the 'aggravating' factors supporting the death penalty and the 'mitigating' factors supporting life imprisonment were equally balanced. The Kansas State Supreme Court ruled that this provision provided a presumption in favour of the death penalty and thereby violated the 8th Amendment ban on 'cruel and unusual punishment'.

> **Extract from 8th Amendment (1791)**
>
> Excessive bail shall not be required, nor excessive fines imposed, nor cruel and unusual punishments inflicted.

Writing for the majority, Justice Clarence Thomas stated that the Kansas death penalty statute 'does not interfere in a constitutionally significant way with a jury's ability to give independent weight to evidence offered in mitigation'. Thomas was joined by his conservative colleagues Scalia, Roberts and Alito as well as by the 'swing justice' Kennedy.

Writing for the minority, Justice David Souter called the Kansas law 'morally absurd' and claimed that Thomas's argument flew in the face of 'decades of precedent aimed at eliminating freakish capital sentencing'. He was joined by his fellow liberal colleagues Stevens, Breyer and Ginsburg. Souter's pronouncements from the bench are usually quiet and understated, but not on this occasion. He used his minority opinion to launch a wider attack on the death penalty as a whole, expressing his doubts of its validity in an era in which DNA evidence had frequently exonerated death row inmates after they had been found guilty. Souter wrote:

> Today, a new body of fact must be accounted for in deciding what, in practical terms, the Eighth Amendment guarantees should tolerate, for the period starting in 1989 has seen repeated exonerations of convicts under death sentences, in numbers never imagined before the development of DNA tests.

Souter backed up this argument with evidence from Illinois, where 13 death row inmates were released between 1977 and 2000, stating that 'false verdicts' are 'probably disproportionately high in capital [punishment] cases'.

Antonin Scalia questioned Souter's argument and use of evidence. He pointed out that a number of prisoners released from death row were released for technical legal reasons, not because they were necessarily innocent. He also cited the case of executed murderer Roger Coleman in Virginia. DNA tests had recently proved that Coleman was guilty, although opponents of capital punishment had earlier claimed that he was wrongly convicted.

Presidential power

Most cases of judicial review involve the Supreme Court declaring unconstitutional laws passed either by the United States Congress or by any of the 50 state congresses. But the power also extends to the Supreme Court declaring unconstitutional actions of the executive branch. This was the category into which the most significant case of the 2005–06 term fell. In the case of *Hamdan* v *Rumsfeld*, the Court declared unconstitutional the military commissions set up by President Bush to try suspected members of Al Qaeda held at Guantánamo Bay in Cuba.

This was a 5–3 decision of the Court: Chief Justice Roberts did not participate because he served on the three-judge Appeal Court panel whose decision to uphold the commissions was being reviewed in this case. If Roberts had participated, one can reasonably assume this would have been another 5–4 decision. The majority opinion was written by Justice Stevens, joined by Breyer, Souter, Ginsburg and Kennedy.

This case will go down as a landmark decision, in which the Supreme Court put a significant limit on the commander-in-chief power of the president, even in time of war and following the attacks on the United States' mainland on 9/11. The Court seemed to be clipping the wings of a president who has employed not only the military commissions that were struck down by this ruling, but also warrantless wiretapping. Thus the broad assertion of presidential power — which has been a hallmark of this Bush administration — has been questioned.

By its decision, the Court seemed to redress the constitutional checks between president and Congress by suggesting that only those tribunals specifically approved by Congress would pass muster with the Court. This was a line of argument pursued by Breyer in a separate majority opinion:

> Where, as here, no emergency prevents consultation with Congress, judicial insistence upon that consultation does not weaken our Nation's ability to deal with danger. To the contrary, that insistence strengthens the Nation's ability to determine — through democratic means — how best to do so. The Constitution places its faith in those democratic means. Our Court today simply does the same.

In his majority opinion, Stevens argued that the Uniform Code of Military Justice (UCMJ) requires that procedures for military commissions should be the same as those for courts martial. But Stevens pointed out that the military tribunals at Guantánamo Bay do not follow these procedures. He also stated that the President's claim of the need for special measures to fight terrorism was not convincing. Stevens therefore ruled the military commissions unconstitutional because they neither followed the UCMJ requirements nor had they been specifically authorised by the Congress. The decision put the ball firmly back in Congress's court.

Two of the three dissenting justices read their opinions from the bench, indicating their strong disapproval of the majority opinion. Scalia argued that the Supreme Court should have stayed out of the case altogether because of the Detainee Treatment Act, passed by Congress in 2005, which laid out appeal rights for those tried by military commissions. Thomas argued that the majority opinion 'openly flouts our well-established duty to respect the Executive's judgement in matters of military operations and foreign affairs'.

According to John McGinnis, a law professor at Northwestern University: 'the mood music of this opinion so lacks the traditional deference to the president that it would seem to have implications for his other programmes.' The Bush administration had claimed that the vote in Congress taken just after the 9/11 attacks, which authorised the President to 'use all necessary and appropriate force' against those who participated in and supported the attacks, gave them the authority to set up the military commissions. But the decision in this case drove a coach and horses through this argument because, in the opinion of John Paul Stevens, 'nothing in the text or legislative history' of that authorising vote 'even hinted that Congress intended to expand or alter' existing laws concerning military trials.

Professor John Yoo, the one-time Bush aide and principal architect of the administration's response to the terrorist threat, claimed that the Court's decision would require the Congress to come up with a laundry list of specific powers before the president could act. 'I wrote that authorisation,' Yoo added in a *New York Times* interview ('The Court enters the war, loudly', 2 July 2006). He continued:

> We wrote it as broadly as possible. In past wars, the Court used to let the president and Congress figure out how to wage the war. That's very different from what's happening today. The Court said, 'If you want to do anything, you have to be very specific and precise about it.'

There is no doubt at all that this line of argument profoundly changes the relationship between the president and Congress, even in wartime. It tilts back the balance in favour of Congress. The Court has in this case given a much more limited interpretation of the president's Article II commander-in-chief powers than the Bush administration would have liked.

Bruce Fein, an official in the Reagan administration, said in a *Washington Post* interview ('A governing philosophy rebuffed', 30 June 2006) that this ruling restores the balances in government. 'What this decision says is, "No, Mr President, you can be bound by treaties and statutes," and if you need to have these changed, you can go to Congress and ask for their permission.' In Fein's view, 'the idea of a coronated president instead of an inaugurated president has been dealt a sharp rebuke'.

The effects of this judgement were on display within hours of the decision being announced. In his first public comments on the case, President Bush declared: 'We've got people looking at it right now to determine how we can work with Congress to solve the problem.' In the view of many of the administration's critics, this is what should have happened 5 years earlier.

Court statistics

In the 2005–06 term the Supreme Court delivered 69 opinions, compared with 74 in the previous term. Of these, 23% were decided by a margin of either 5–4 or 5–3, compared with 30% in 2004–05 (see Table 3.2). The justice most frequently in the majority during the 2005–06 term was Chief Justice John Roberts, a hint at the rightward shift of the Court during this term. In the 2004–05 term that distinction had gone to Clinton appointee Stephen Breyer. In this term, Breyer had the second highest number of *dissenting* opinions. That said, Breyer was on the winning side in the landmark *Hamdan* decision and authored the majority opinion in the important campaign finance decision.

	2000–01	2001–02	2002–03	2003–04	2004–05	2005–06
Number of cases	77	79	71	73	74	69
Decided by 5–4 majority	32%	27%	20%	25%	30%	23%
Justice most frequently in majority	O'Connor	O'Connor/ Rehnquist	O'Connor	O'Connor	Breyer	Roberts

Table 3.2 Supreme Court statistics, 2000–06

The two justices with the highest agreement rate were the two new Bush appointees, Chief Justice Roberts and Associate Justice Alito. They agreed on 88% of non-unanimous cases. Next most often in agreement were O'Connor and Souter. This statistic demonstrates how significant the Alito for O'Connor switch has been. Chief Justice Roberts agreed with Scalia — arguably the Court's most conservative jurist — in 77.5% of non-unanimous cases, while he agreed with Stevens — arguably the Court's most liberal member — in only 35% of such cases. The least agreement between a pair of justices was between Alito and Stevens — further indications of Alito's conservative credentials.

The Roberts Court

It is too early to discern what the Roberts Court will look like. A lot may depend on who gets to make the replacement for Justice Stevens, the Court's leading liberal, as and when he decides to retire from the Court. But even in this first year, Roberts seemed to be laying out his stall as a conservative, albeit a more restrained conservative. Perhaps as a reaction to some adverse public opinion to the Court's involvement in the result of the 2000 presidential election, the new Chief Justice is trying to give the Court, in the words of the first President Bush, a 'kinder, gentler' face.

In a little-reported speech at Georgetown University Law School in May 2006, Roberts stated that 'if it is not necessary to decide more to dispose of a case, in my view it is necessary not to decide more'. In this, Roberts appeared to be suggesting a more minimalist, restrained role for the Supreme Court. As E. J. Dionne put it in his comment column in the *Washington Post* ('The Chief Justice sets a standard', 20 June 2006, p. A17), Roberts seemed to be saying 'the less the Court decides the better'.

Roberts also appeared to be suggesting that as Chief Justice he would be reaching out to other members of the Court and trying to gain as many votes as possible for any particular decision. He might be able to get a 5–4 majority, but he would prefer to compromise his views a little to gain a 6–3 or greater majority if that were possible. 'The rule of law is strengthened when there is greater coherence and agreement about what the law is,' stated Roberts in his Georgetown lecture.

There were times in his first term when Roberts did not seem to heed his own advice; the 5–4 decision in *Hudson* v *Michigan* comes to mind. But according to E. J. Dionne: '…if Roberts lives up to his Georgetown principles, he will justify all the votes cast for his confirmation by moderates and liberals. More importantly, he will win a place in history as the chief justice who ended the judicial wars.' No mean achievement.

Chapter 4

Bush and Congress: the first 6 years

What you need to know
- The powers of the president are significantly checked by Congress.
- Congress can delay, amend or reject the legislation the president recommends to them.
- Congress can override the president's veto.
- Congress can hold investigations into the policies pursued by the president.
- Congress has the power to impeach and try the president.
- The Senate can reject appointments that the president makes to both the executive and the judiciary.
- The Senate can refuse to ratify treaties negotiated by the president.
- The president's party may not always be the majority party in both houses of Congress.
- The president often has to rely on his powers of persuasion to get his way in Congress.

Factors that affect presidential success in Congress

During his first 6 years in office, President George W. Bush possessed one significant advantage in his dealings with Congress that his immediate predecessors did not have — party control of both houses of Congress. True, his party — the Republicans — did lose control of the Senate for an 18-month period in 2001–02, but for the remainder of his first 6 years in office, President Bush enjoyed comfortable Republican majorities in both the House of Representatives and the Senate.

During Bill Clinton's 8 years in office (1993–2001) he had party control of Congress for only 2 years. The current president's father, George H. W. Bush (1989–93) did not have his own party in the majority in either house during his term in office. Before that, Republican Ronald Reagan (1981–89) enjoyed a Republican majority in the Senate for his first 6 years but never controlled the House of Representatives. George W. Bush has experienced a coincidence of party control in Congress not seen since the days of Lyndon Johnson (1963–69). This puts him at a significant advantage when dealing with Congress.

Bush also had the advantage of stratospherically high approval ratings in the months immediately after the attacks on America on 11 September 2001. High approval ratings for the president always increase his political clout — politicians want to follow a winner more than a loser. And as President Bush's approval ratings have fallen away during his second term, so has his ability to get things done in Congress.

Party control and public approval ratings are two important factors that affect a president's ability to be successful in Congress. But there are others. The margin of victory at election or re-election is another important factor. If the president wins big (like Johnson in 1964) or is re-elected by a huge margin (like Reagan in 1984), presidents tend to find that success comes more easily. Likewise, presidents who win only by small margins (like Carter in 1976) often find success harder to come by. Bill Clinton did not achieve 50% of the popular vote in either of his two elections. In 2000, George W. Bush failed to win the popular vote, even though he became president! Even his winning margin in 2004 was quite narrow.

It is often thought that presidents who are Washington insiders — those who have served in Congress, or elsewhere in the federal government — find it easier to achieve success in Congress than Washington outsiders. Lyndon Johnson and Richard Nixon had not only both served in Congress but had also acted as vice-president before coming to the presidency. George W. Bush follows in the footsteps of Carter, Reagan and Clinton as a Washington outsider. He has subsequently depended more on others in his administration to deliver success in Congress. Most important in this respect during these first 6 years were Vice-President Dick Cheney and White House Chief of Staff Andrew Card. Both had distinguished Washington careers before joining the Bush administration in 2001.

Measuring presidential success in Congress

One way in which scholars and commentators of the presidency measure presidential success in Congress is through the annual presidential support score. This score measures how often a president wins in recorded votes in the House and the Senate in which he took a clear position, expressed as a percentage. The score has been calculated and published by *Congressional Quarterly* — a well-respected Washington journal — since 1953. The average support score in the years between 1953 and when George W. Bush came to office in 2001 was 67%. The highest annual support score was 93.1% (Johnson, 1965) and the lowest was 36.2% (Clinton, 1995).

Year	Presidential support score (%)
2001	87.0
2002	87.8
2003	78.7
2004	72.6
2005	78.0

Table 4.1 Presidential support score for George W. Bush, 2001–05

Table 4.1 shows that in his first 5 years as president, Bush was well above average. Indeed, his average score during this period was just under 81%, less than two percentage points away from Johnson's record of 82.6% over 5 years. In 2005, Bush set a new record high for a president in his fifth year of office — 78% — beating Johnson's 74.5% in 1968 (see Table 4.2).

President	Year	Presidential support score (%)
George W. Bush	2005	78.0
Lyndon Johnson	1968	74.5
Dwight Eisenhower	1957	68.4
Ronald Reagan	1985	59.9
Bill Clinton	1997	53.6
Richard Nixon	1973	50.6

Table 4.2 Presidential support score for presidents in their fifth year of office, 1957–2005

Although this score is a useful guide to presidential success in Congress, there are ways in which it can tell less than the whole story. A president may seek to boost his score by taking fewer public positions on votes in Congress. This may be a tactic that Bush has used to his advantage, as he has taken a position on fewer congressional votes than any of his immediate predecessors. In 2005, for example, Bush took a definite position on only 46 of the 669 recorded votes in the House of Representatives and on only 45 of the 366 votes in the Senate. This means that Bush took a position on just 91 out of 1,035 votes in Congress, the lowest figure since 1972. In comparison, Bill Clinton took a position on 235 votes in 1995 and Jimmy Carter took a position on 306 votes in 1979.

Bush's key legislative victories

The 107th Congress (2001–02)

Although Bush was a Washington outsider and the loser of the popular vote in 2000, presidential scholar Michael Nelson has noted that he entered the White House in 2001 with two advantages that most of his predecessors had lacked ('George W. Bush and Congress', in G. L. Gregg and M. J. Rozell *Considering the Bush Presidency*, Oxford University Press, 2004). First, as governor of Texas he had experience of working cooperatively with a strong state legislature controlled by the opposition party. As a Republican in a still predominantly Democratic state, Bush had to work with Texas Democrats to get things done. Jimmy Carter and Bill Clinton came from states where the legislature was both weak and controlled by their own party. Bush's second advantage was that his party enjoyed a nine-seat majority in the House and a one-seat working majority in the Senate, thanks to Vice-President Cheney's casting vote in a Senate divided 50–50 between Democrats and Republicans.

Throughout the 107th Congress, Bush's approach to Congress resembled the approach he had taken towards the state legislature in Texas: outline his goals in broad terms, allow Congress to work its will, then claim whatever compromise emerges as a victory. This strategy was seen clearly in his signature victory of the 107th Congress: education reform. Despite dropping his education voucher scheme, Bush signed the bill and then embarked on a nationwide tour to tout his success.

Bush also persuaded Congress to pass a bill to cut federal taxes by $1.35 trillion over 10 years. As with the education reform bill, Bush achieved his success by gaining the votes of some moderate Democrats. In the House, the bill was passed 230–197. All 216 Republicans voted for it, plus 13 Democrats and the Independent (soon to switch to the Republicans) Virgil Goode of Virginia. In the Senate the margin was 62–38, with all 50 Republicans voting 'yes', plus 12 Democrats.

Bush's other legislative successes of the 107th Congress came after 9/11 when Congress passed by huge majorities a number of bills relating to domestic security. A post-9/11 $40 billion recovery package was passed by the House 408–6 and the Senate 94–2. A bill placing airport security under federal government control was passed unanimously by the Senate and with only nine dissenting votes in the House.

But there were a number of areas in which Congress failed to act. The President had, for example, wanted congressional action on an overhaul of bankruptcy legislation and the provision of prescription drugs under the Medicare system. These and other pieces of presidential-supported legislation fell by the wayside.

The 108th Congress (2003–04)

The 2002 mid-term elections were a significant personal boost for President Bush. He became the first president to gain seats in both houses of Congress in a mid-term election since Franklin Roosevelt in 1934. Bush's Republicans picked up 5 House seats and 2 Senate seats following a huge amount of campaigning by the President in support of Republican candidates. In the last 5 days of the campaign, the President travelled 16,000 kilometres, visiting 17 cities in 15 states. 'The blitz was a major, and perhaps determining, factor in several key elections,' commented *Congressional Quarterly*'s Bob Benenson.

Thus Bush came out of the 2002 mid-term elections having regained control of the Senate and with his standing sky-high within the Republican congressional caucus. But his support was quickly sapped by two seemingly minor events. First, the Republicans lost a Senate run-off election in Louisiana the following month. 'The Bush political juggernaut was not irresistible,' commented Michael Nelson. Second, the Republican leader in the Senate, Trent Lott of Mississippi, was forced to resign his leadership position following some racially insensitive remarks he made at a 100th birthday party for Senator Strom Thurmond.

While Bush was highly successful in the foreign policy arena — most notably in the toppling of Saddam Hussein's government in Iraq in the spring of 2003 — his domestic policy agenda languished. He lost an important vote on oil drilling in Alaska when a number of moderate Republicans voted with the Democrats. More significantly, Bush saw several of his more conservative judicial nominees filibustered by Senate Democrats, with Republicans unable to garner the necessary votes to bring the obstruction to an end. Bush claimed a $350 billion tax cut as a victory despite having originally asked Congress for a cut of $726 billion. 'Sometimes I get everything I want, sometimes I don't,' the President told lawmakers at a gathering at the White House. Presidential spokesman Ari Fleischer commented: 'The President is getting less than he would have liked. He recognises that. He wishes it could have been more. But he is pleased, nevertheless, that a compromise has been reached.' Meanwhile, Bush's proposals on medical malpractice and welfare reform were put on the congressional 'back burner'.

During these 2 years, Bush was not helped by the fact that a number of leading Democrat senators — John Kerry of Massachusetts, John Edwards of North Carolina, Bob Graham of Florida and Joe Lieberman of Connecticut — were seeking to become their party's nominee for the presidency to oppose Bush in November 2004. Neither they nor their fellow Democrats were about to deliver a string of legislative successes to the President on the eve of his re-election bid. And once John Kerry had wrapped up the nomination in spring 2004 the Senate virtually ground to a halt as far as President Bush's agenda was concerned.

The 109th Congress (2005–06)

Bush's big wins in 2005 came in the enactment of his long sought-after limits on class action lawsuits and bankruptcy filings, an energy bill, a highway and transit bill and the Central American Free Trade Agreement. The President also had a more profitable time with the Senate in terms of getting his judicial nominations approved. His nominee for Chief Justice of the Supreme Court, John Roberts, was confirmed by a bipartisan majority of 78 votes to 22, with 22 Democrats and 1 Independent joining all 55 Republicans to confirm the President's nominee.

But the 109th Congress was also marked by defeats, compromises and setbacks for the President. He had to undergo a complete about-face when accepting Senator John McCain's legislation on the use of torture against US terrorist detainees. He was forced to retreat again over the renewal of the 2001 Patriot Act. But the biggest retreat of all came in the withdrawal of the nomination of Harriet Miers, the President's own White House legal counsel, to the Supreme Court. This was forced on the President not by opposition from Democrats but from conservative Republicans who were unconvinced of Miers' conservative credentials. This was in addition to the Senate's refusal to confirm John Bolton as American ambassador to the United Nations: the President had to resort to his recess appointment power to install Bolton at the UN until January 2007.

The second session of the 109th Congress (2006) saw the confirmation of Samuel Alito to the US Supreme Court to replace Sandra Day O'Connor. This was a clear win for the President, in that it seemed to mark a rightward shift in the ideology of the Court.

The session also witnessed the President's first use of his veto power. For 5 years Bush had not used a presidential veto, making him the first president since John Quincy Adams (1825–29) to go through a full 4-year term without using a veto. The bill that Bush vetoed was one that would have removed existing limits on federal funding for stem cell research. The bill had not experienced an easy passage through the legislative process. The House had passed its version of the bill in May 2005 by 238 votes to 194, a vote that had fractured party lines. The 'yes' votes were made up of 187 Democrats, 50 Republicans and Independent Bernie Sanders, while the 'no' votes were cast by 180 Republicans and 14 Democrats. It was the President's own party that was most divided on the issue. Many Republicans oppose stem cell research for the same reasons that they oppose abortion — reasons concerning the sanctity of human life.

It took over a year of negotiations before Senate Majority Leader Bill Frist was able to bring the bill to the floor of his chamber. The Senate eventually passed the bill 63–37, four votes short of the two-thirds majority that would be required to override the President's veto. In the Senate, the 'yes' votes were cast by 43 Democrats, 19 Republicans and Independent James Jeffords. The 'no' votes were those of 36 Republicans and one Democrat.

The Republican 'no' votes in the Senate were cast by quite an ideological range of senators. It was no surprise to see such names as John McCain of Arizona, Olympia Snowe and Susan Collins of Maine, Lincoln Chafee of Rhode Island and Arlen Specter of Pennsylvania — all noted mavericks or moderates. But they were joined by such conservative Republicans as Trent Lott of Mississippi, and Orrin Hatch and Robert Bennett of Utah. The lone Democrat 'no' vote was cast by Ben Nelson of Nebraska, who was facing a tough re-election race later in the year.

The Senate voted on 18 July and the President vetoed the bill on 19 July. Later the same day, the House voted to override the President's veto but, requiring a two-thirds majority, the attempt failed: the result was 235–193, 51 votes short of the 286 votes required to override the veto. In the debate before the override vote, House Majority Leader John Boehner urged his colleagues to sustain the President's veto. 'No just society should condone destruction of innocent life, even in the name of medical research,' he stated. 'The President was right to veto this bill.' Fellow Republican Thomas Davis of Virginia disagreed. In justifying going against both his congressional leadership and his president, Davis stated:

> I'm going to vote to override [the veto] just because it's hard to look the mother of a child with juvenile diabetes or someone whose parent has Alzheimer's in the eye, and not let them know I'm doing everything I can in my elected position to help them.

Bush's veto record

Bush used his veto power for the first time on 19 July 2006, almost exactly $5\frac{1}{2}$ years after taking the oath of office on 20 January 2001. As stated above, Bush waited longer than any president since the 1820s to use his veto power. The question therefore arises as to why this was. Why this unusually long period of time without using the ultimate power that the Constitution grants to the president in his dealings with Congress? What is more, it is a power that presidents invariably wield successfully. Over 218 years, presidents have used their regular veto against 1,485 bills. Of these, Congress has passed into law — by overriding that veto — only 106 bills, just 7% of all vetoed bills. In other words, presidents won on 93% of vetoes — quite a success rate! So why not use it?

First, presidents who have party control of Congress tend to use the veto far less frequently than those who face divided government. Bush's predecessor Bill Clinton (1993–2001) did not use a single veto during the 2 years in which his fellow Democrats controlled both houses of Congress. He then vetoed 36 bills during the following 6 years, when the Republicans were running Congress. However, Jimmy Carter (1977–81) used his regular veto 13 times, despite having his own party in control of both houses of Congress. So the fact that Bush has enjoyed control of the House for all of his first 6 years and the Senate for $4\frac{1}{2}$ of the first 6 years is likely to be a factor in his reluctance to use the veto.

Second, it is probably true to say that Bush has a more limited legislative agenda than most of his more recent predecessors — certainly more so than his immediate predecessor, Bill Clinton. While Clinton's legislative agenda resembled a child's Christmas present wish list, Bush's agenda could be written on a postage stamp. For Bush, unless it is education reform, tax cuts or the 'war on terror', he has not shown himself to be that committed. Witness the few votes in Congress upon which he has taken a position, as observed earlier in this chapter.

Third, Bush is a compromiser. When Clinton wanted to push his healthcare proposals in Congress in his 1994 State of the Union Address, he theatrically brandished a pen during the speech, saying that he would veto any bill that did not contain 100% healthcare coverage. No compromise there. But then by the end of the year there would be no healthcare reform bill either. Clinton's lack of willingness to compromise meant that he could not attract the votes of some moderate Republicans, which he needed in order to get the bill passed. Alistair Cooke once observed that American government is based on three fundamental principles — 'compromise, compromise and compromise'. Bush is quite happy to switch horses during the race, even proclaiming what seem to be defeats as principled victories — witness his reaction to Congress's limited renewal of the Patriot Act in 2005.

Fourth, congressional Republicans have been extremely accommodating to their president, far more so than congressional Democrats were to either Bill Clinton or Jimmy Carter. Republican leaders in both chambers have often delayed votes on bills until they could be sure of passing a bill that would find favour with the White House. However, the relationship has not been all one sided. John Cranford wrote in *Congressional Quarterly* (24 July 2006) that 'Bush's dealings with Capitol Hill have been far less confrontational than the other presidents in the last half-century.' Bush has also used the threat of a veto to good effect. In the final negotiations for an omnibus spending bill in 2004, the President threatened a veto and Congress backed off from using the bill to lift a travel and trade ban on Cuba.

Finally, George W. Bush has for much of his presidency had high public approval ratings. That always helps to increase the clout of the president. As these numbers have waned, however — especially since his re-election — Bush finds that Congress is increasingly reluctant to practise 'followership' to his leadership. As he enters the last 2 years of his final term, he will increasingly be seen as a 'lame duck' president. UK Prime Minister Tony Blair repeatedly refused to name the precise date of his departure, lest his authority drain away even more than it already has. The US president has no such luxury, for everyone knows that at 12 noon on 20 January 2009, President George W. Bush will bow out. The President has little time — and maybe even less opportunity — to burnish his legislative legacy.

Chapter 5
The 2008 Presidential election

What you need to know
- Presidential elections occur every 4 years.
- Presidents are limited to two 4-year terms in office.
- Both major parties hold a series of state-based primaries and caucuses during the first 5 months of the election year.
- Primaries and caucuses give ordinary voters a chance to say who they would like to see as the parties' presidential candidates.
- The 'invisible primary' is the period before the primaries and caucuses when would-be candidates try to position themselves for the race, gain name recognition and media attention, as well as raise large amounts of money.
- The candidate of each party who is ahead in the opinion polls at the end of the 'invisible primary' usually ends up as the party's presidential candidate.

Year	Republican candidate	Democrat candidate
1952	General Dwight Eisenhower	Governor Adlai Stevenson
1956	**President Dwight Eisenhower**	Governor Adlai Stevenson
1960	**Vice-President Richard Nixon**	Senator John Kennedy
1964	Senator Barry Goldwater	**President Lyndon Johnson**
1968	Former Vice-President Richard Nixon	**Vice-President Hubert Humphrey**
1972	**President Richard Nixon**	Senator George McGovern
1976	**President Gerald Ford**	Governor Jimmy Carter
1980	Governor Ronald Reagan	**President Jimmy Carter**
1984	**President Ronald Reagan**	Former Vice-President Walter Mondale
1988	**Vice-President George Bush**	Governor Michael Dukakis
1992	**President George Bush**	Governor Bill Clinton
1996	Senator Bob Dole	**President Bill Clinton**
2000	Governor George W. Bush	**Vice-President Al Gore**
2004	**President George W. Bush**	Senator John Kerry

Table 5.1 Republican and Democrat presidential candidates, 1952–2004 (incumbent presidents and vice-presidents in bold)

The 2006 mid-term elections are over, so the focus of American politics now switches to the presidential election of 2008. With President Bush ineligible for re-election, having already served two terms, and Vice-President Dick Cheney

Annual Survey, 2007

Year	Presidential/vice-presidential candidates
1948	Thomas Dewey/Earl Warren
1952	Dwight Eisenhower/**Richard Nixon**
1956	Dwight Eisenhower/**Richard Nixon**
1960	**Richard Nixon**/Henry Cabot Lodge
1964	Barry Goldwater/William Miller
1968	**Richard Nixon**/Spiro Agnew
1972	**Richard Nixon**/Spiro Agnew
1976	Gerald Ford/**Bob Dole**
1980	Ronald Reagan/**George Bush**
1984	Ronald Reagan/**George Bush**
1988	**George Bush**/Dan Quayle
1992	**George Bush**/Dan Quayle
1996	**Bob Dole**/Jack Kemp
2000	**George W. Bush**/Dick Cheney
2004	**George W. Bush**/Dick Cheney

Table 5.2 Republican presidential and vice-presidential candidates, 1948–2004

showing no interest in running, the race for the White House in 2008 will be unusually open. As Table 5.1 shows, the last presidential race that did not feature the incumbent president or vice-president was in 1952. The Republicans are also likely to set another record, for 2008 is likely to be only the second presidential election since 1948 that will not feature a presidential or vice-presidential candidate named Nixon, Dole or Bush (see Table 5.2). The other was in 1964 when the Republican ticket was Barry Goldwater and William Miller. This is quite a record in a nation that is supposed to eschew political dynasties.

With both major parties having an open field for 2008, it is not surprising to find a large crop of potential candidates on both sides of the political divide. But another situation that might occur in 2008 is the return of the Washington insider candidate. In the last eight elections — those between 1976 and 2004 — the only presidential candidates who won as challengers rather than incumbents were all state governors: Governor Carter (1976), Governor Reagan (1980), Governor Clinton (1992) and Governor Bush (2000). Not since 1960 has a Washington insider challenged the presidency and won — Senator John Kennedy. In over 40 years since Kennedy was elected, four incumbent senators have been nominated for the presidency by the major parties. All four lost — Senator Goldwater (1964), Senator McGovern (1972), Senator Dole (1996) and Senator Kerry (2004). However, the 2008 field of would-be presidential candidates is dominated by Senators rather than state governors. In the era of global terrorism and with the focus on foreign wars, are American voters looking for Washington experience rather than taking on another Washington outsider? Have Clinton and Bush's lack of Washington savvy finally done it in — at least temporarily — for the state governor-turned president?

Why 2008 looks like the Democrats' year

With the incumbent Republican president ineligible for re-election and the incumbent vice-president uninterested in running, the Democrats will undoubtedly be thinking that they stand a good chance of winning the White House in 2008. There are two reasons for this. First, George W. Bush is likely to end his term of office as relatively unpopular. Second, the twentieth century witnessed only three occasions when a president was succeeded by a president of his own party through election. This occurred in 1908 when Teddy

Roosevelt was followed by William Howard Taft, in 1928 when Calvin Coolidge was followed by Herbert Hoover, and in 1988 when Ronald Reagan was followed by George Bush — all, incidentally, Republicans. On most occasions when an incumbent president was not taking part in the election — 1920, 1952, 1960, 1968 and 2000 — there was a switch of parties. In other words, of the eight takeovers of the White House during the last century, only three were 'friendly' while five were 'hostile' (see Table 5.3).

Year	President	Party	Followed by	Party
1908	Teddy Roosevelt	R	William Howard Taft	R
1920	Woodrow Wilson	D	Warren Harding	R
1928	Calvin Coolidge	R	Herbert Hoover	R
1952	Harry Truman	D	Dwight Eisenhower	R
1960	Dwight Eisenhower	R	John Kennedy	D
1968	Lyndon Johnson	D	Richard Nixon	R
1988	Ronald Reagan	R	George Bush	R
2000	Bill Clinton	D	George W. Bush	R

Table 5.3 Friendly and hostile takeovers of the White House since 1908

More changes in the nominating calendar

Often in the past when the Democrats have lost the race for the White House, they have sought to make changes to the calendar by which they select their presidential candidate. This occurred most spectacularly after the 1968 defeat of Democrat Hubert Humphrey, when the Democrats established the McGovern-Fraser Commission to draw up new rules for selecting presidential candidates. Then, after the defeat of Jimmy Carter in 1980, there was the Hunt Commission, which introduced 'super delegates' to the National Party Convention.

After their defeat in 2004, the Democrats were at it again with another committee to take a fresh look at the presidential nominating process. Some Democrats were concerned at the speed with which Senator John Kerry of Massachusetts wrapped up the presidential nomination in 2004, following the spectacular collapse of the campaign of the initial front-runner, Governor Howard Dean of Vermont. Commentators had talked of 'buyers' regret' — buying something from a shop on impulse, but then regretting the purchase after a few days when the item does not match up to the initial promise. It was felt, therefore, that a more reflective process — one that lasted rather longer and featured a better variety of more representative states — would be an advantage. The present front loaded system (in which lots of states cram their primaries and caucuses into a few weeks in February and March, dominated by such quirky states as Iowa and New Hampshire), is thought by some to be an unhelpful way of choosing the presidential candidate.

In July 2006, the Democratic National Committee received a report from the Rules and Bylaws Committee, which they had set up to recommend reforms of the nominating system. The committee made a number of proposals. First, Democrats in Nevada would be invited to hold caucuses 5 days after the caucuses in Iowa — the state that traditionally kicks off the nominating calendar. Second, Democrats in South Carolina would be invited to hold a primary 1 week after the New Hampshire primary, which is traditionally the first primary. The purpose behind these two proposals was to introduce two more representative states from different parts of the country, in an attempt to reduce the over-importance of Iowa and New Hampshire. Nevada is a fast-growing western state where Hispanics make up 20% of the population. South Carolina is an important southern state where black people make up 30% of the population. The idea was that these two states would balance the influence of small, rural, overwhelmingly white Iowa and New Hampshire. It is expected that these proposals will be implemented for 2008.

National Conventions

The dates for the 2008 National Party Conventions have already been announced. Traditionally, the challenging party (the Democrats in 2008) hold their convention first, and this is what will happen this time around. What is unusual is that the two conventions have been scheduled very close to each other. The Democrats are holding their convention in the week beginning 25 August 2008, and the Republicans follow just 1 week later on 1 September.

The Republicans were the first to announce the venue of their convention: Minneapolis and St Paul in the Great Lakes state of Minnesota. This is a first for the Republicans in the 'Twin Cities', as they are known. Minnesota is a traditional Democratic state into which the Republicans have recently been making inroads. Norm Coleman is a Republican senator from Minnesota and the Republicans now hold three of the eight seats in the House of Representatives. In 1992, President George H. W. Bush polled just 31% for the Republicans in Minnesota. In 2004, his son polled nearly 48%. The Republicans are hoping to appeal to Twin City suburban voters, and thus possibly swing Minnesota into the Republican column for only the second time since 1960. (President Nixon won Minnesota in his 49-state sweep in 1972.)

The Democrats have yet to announce their convention venue. They had also been considering Minneapolis-St Paul, but have now taken it off their shortlist, given the closeness in dates of the two conventions. The smart money is on the Democrats going to Denver, Colorado. Like the Republicans in Minnesota, the Democrats have seen their fortunes rising in Colorado in recent elections, partly due to a growing Hispanic population. They now have a Democrat senator, Ken Salazar, one of three Hispanic members in the Senate during the 109th Congress (2005–06). In 2004, the Democratic ticket of John Kerry and John Edwards won 47% of the vote in Colorado.

The would-be presidential candidates

I'm often asked 'will Hillary Clinton be the next president of the United States?' Writing this in the autumn of 2006, it would be a brave person who would attempt to identify the presidential candidates in 2008, let alone state who might come out as the winner. Who in the autumn of 1990 would have identified Bill Clinton as the next president of the United States? All we can do this far away is to identify some of the likely candidates.

Likely Republican candidates	Likely Democrat candidates
Senator John McCain	Senator Hillary Clinton
Former Mayor Rudolph Giuliani	Senator Evan Bayh
Former Governor Mitt Romney	Former Senator John Edwards
	Former Vice-President Al Gore
	Former Governor Tom Vilsack

Table 5.4 Likely presidential candidates for 2008

The likely Republican candidates

There seem to be three serious contenders for the 2008 Republican presidential nomination: one senator, one ex-city mayor and one ex-state governor.

The front-runner at present appears to be Senator **John McCain** of Arizona. It was McCain who mounted a serious challenge to George W. Bush for the Republican nomination in 2000, but Bush had all of his father's organisational contacts. McCain was first elected to the Senate in 1986 and was re-elected to a third term in 2004 with 76% of the vote. According to Michael Barone in the *Almanac of American Politics*: 'For many Americans John McCain is the closest thing our politics has to a national hero.' McCain's compelling autobiography, *Faith of My Fathers*, tells the story of being shot down over Vietnam and spending 5 years, most of it in pain and under torture, in Communist POW camps. McCain is a maverick, frequently out of favour with his Senate colleagues and even the Bush White House. His single-minded pursuit of campaign finance reform legislation is his most significant legislative achievement, with the passage of the Bipartisan Campaign Reform Act in 2002. McCain's strength would be his appeal to independent voters. The major problem he faces is his lack of support among conservative Republican voters — just the ones who tend to turn out for the primaries. He would also have to face the age issue: he will be 72 by election day, 3 years older than Ronald Reagan was when he was first elected to the presidency in 1980.

Former New York Mayor **Rudolph Giuliani** won his place in national folklore on 11 September 2001, with his courageous and unruffled response to the terrible events of that day. Unlike any other former city mayor, Giuliani enjoys huge name recognition. But anyone who can get elected in the city of New York is likely to struggle to win the hearts and minds of conservative

Republicans in the Bible Belt. Giuliani will be viewed as far too liberal by many Republicans. Given that Republican primary election voters tend to be even more conservative than Republican general election voters, he faces a huge uphill battle to succeed in the Republican primaries.

The Republican dark horse of 2008 might be the former Governor of Massachusetts, **Mitt Romney**. Romney is a highly intellectual and personable politician. He comes from a famous political family: his father, George Romney, was Governor of Michigan from 1963 to 1969 and then served 4 years in President Nixon's cabinet as Secretary of Housing and Urban Development. To be elected as a Republican in Massachusetts is a remarkable achievement. The state's two senators are the liberal war horses Ted Kennedy and John Kerry, and all of its ten-member House delegation are Democrats. There are only 29 Republicans in the 200-member state legislature. But Romney has been popular and successful as governor, turning around a huge budget deficit into a surplus in his 4-year term. He will need to overcome one potentially significant hurdle: his religion. Romney, who lived much of his adult life in Utah, is a Mormon. A significant proportion of American voters have told pollsters that they would not vote for a Mormon as their president. But then in 1960, a similarly sizable minority said the same thing about voting for a presidential candidate who was a Catholic. Yet Catholic John Kennedy won that year's election.

The likely Democratic candidates

One can also identify five serious contenders for the 2008 Democratic presidential nomination: two senators, a former senator, a former vice-president and a former state governor.

The front-runner for the Democrats at present seems to be Senator **Hillary Clinton**, the junior senator from New York and former First Lady. She has name recognition, organisational connections and fundraising potential. She has spent the last 6 years burnishing her reputation as a handy Washington operative, quietly beavering away in the Senate on behalf of her adopted state of New York. Even Republican colleagues have grudgingly given her admiring reviews. But Clinton is also a divisive character and could therefore be a divisive candidate. In the South, she will be seen by many as little more than John Kerry in a skirt — another liberal senator from a northeastern state. Her Senate vote in favour of the Iraq war back in 2002 may yet prove problematic for her. In any presidential campaign, she would have to decide how to cope with her husband. Hillary Clinton once famously said that as First Lady she would not 'stay home and bake cookies'. As potential First Husband, Mr Clinton would certainly not be content with cookie baking either. But could the former president play a number two role, even in a campaign? Would his energetic and exuberant campaigning and speech-making merely make his wife look rather wooden?

Another serving senator who may feature strongly in 2008 is the junior senator from Indiana, **Evan Bayh**. Senator Bayh (it is pronounced 'by') has considerable political experience — he served 10 years as the state's governor from 1986 to 1996 before being elected to the Senate in 1998. He was re-elected to a second term in 2004 with a whopping 62% of the vote in a red state that President Bush won with 60% of the vote. Like Mitt Romney, Evan Bayh has a famous father — Senator Birch Bayh, who for 36 years occupied the same seat that his son now holds. His father ran for president in 1976, losing in the Democratic primaries to Governor Jimmy Carter. Will we see a re-run of the 1976 newspaper headlines 'Bye-bye Bayh'?

Hoping for a wheel or two to come off the Hillary Clinton bandwagon will be former Senator **John Edwards** of North Carolina, the 2004 Democratic vice-presidential candidate. Edwards has spent the last 3 years preparing for a presidential bid. But his political experience is limited to just one term in the Senate. Will that be the kind of experience that voters will be looking for in the uncertain times that are likely to beset America at election time? Probably not. True, Edwards would be more palatable to southern voters than Hillary Clinton, but does he have a truly national appeal? Clinton may be rather lifeless, but that's better than being lightweight — the adjective most often attached to Edwards.

Will **Al Gore** do a Richard Nixon? Nixon served 8 years as vice-president to Dwight Eisenhower in the 1950s and then when Eisenhower was term-limited in 1960, Nixon ran as the party's candidate, losing in a close race to John F. Kennedy. Eight years later, Nixon was back and won the presidency. In a similar way, Gore served as vice-president to Bill Clinton in the 1990s and then when Clinton was term-limited in 2000, he ran as the party's candidate, losing in a very close race to George W. Bush. Gore has a lot of baggage to overcome. He would have to convince his party that although he lost in 2000 against the backdrop of prosperity at home and peace abroad — and lost to an opponent widely perceived as flawed — he is worthy of another chance. An election cycle dominated by Clinton and Gore once again is perhaps not an appetising thought — shades of 1992, 1996 and 2000?

The Democrats, too, have a former state Governor lurking in the wings: **Tom Vilsack** of Iowa. The former mayor of Mount Pleasant and member of the Iowa state Senate was first elected Governor in 1998 and was term-limited in 2006. Vilsack has proved a successful governor, despite having to work with a state legislature in which both houses are controlled by Republicans. But his name recognition outside the Midwest is pretty limited. Against names like Clinton and Gore, he's got a tough assignment. Having said that, so did another little-known state Governor — Jimmy Carter — in 1976. And look what happened to him.

The others

Having singled out nine would-be presidential candidates, I still wonder whether I might not have named the next president of the United States. What about **Condoleezza Rice** for the Republicans? Severely embarrassed by allegations of incompetence in a recently published book by Bob Woodward, Dr Rice would certainly bring interest to the campaign. Then there's the former Republican Governor of New York, **George Pataki**. Former New York governors have included Franklin Roosevelt and Nelson Rockefeller, who went on to become president and vice-president respectively. Could Pataki follow in their footsteps?

On the Democrats' side, there is Senator **John Kerry** of Massachusetts. Does he fancy another bid? Or how about fellow senators **Joe Biden** of Delaware, **Christopher Dodd** of Connecticut or **Barack Obama** of Illinois? Then there's Governor **Bill Richardson** of New Mexico, a former member of the House of Representatives and of Bill Clinton's cabinet.

The lists go on and on, and with 2 years to run, the presidential election campaign — from invisible primary to election night — is likely to do the same.

Chapter 6
The red and blue debate revisited

In the 2006 edition we looked at the red state–blue state debate, which has come to dominate much of the commentary about American politics in the first decade of the twenty-first century. The terminology is drawn from the colours used by the media to denote states won by the Republicans (red) and the Democrats (blue) in presidential elections. Many commentators have looked at maps from 2000 and 2004, with their oceans of red and islands of blue, and concluded that America is deeply divided — what has been called a '50–50 nation'.

The media, as well as many political scientists, seem to have bought into the red v blue debate and see contemporary American politics in this light. America is portrayed as a divided nation, characterised by increased levels of polarisation and partisanship. According to them, the nation is gripped in a 'culture war', with a devout south and Midwest 'at war' with a secular northeast and west coast.

The 50–50 nation thesis

At the 1992 Republican National Convention, the conservative commentator Pat Buchanan gave voice to the views he had espoused with limited success in that year's Republican primaries. While the first President Bush was talking about a 'kinder, gentler' America, Buchanan let fly with both barrels. 'There is a religious war going in this country, a cultural war as critical to the kind of nation we shall be as the Cold War itself, for this war is for the soul of America.' I remember spending time the following year with a moderate Republican Congressman from New Mexico, the late Steve Schiff. Asked at a public meeting what he had thought of Buchanan's speech, the usually mild mannered Schiff waspishly replied: 'I didn't hear it, but I have read the translation from the original German!'

The numerical justification for the term 'the 50–50 nation' is drawn from the figures shown in Table 6.1 — that in many elections over the past decade, America seems to have been split 50–50. The 50–50 nation thesis has

Year/election	Percentage of the vote
1996: Bill Clinton's re-election	49.2
1996: Republican House vote	48.9
1998: Republican House vote	48.9
2000: Al Gore's vote	48.4
2000: Republican House vote	48.3
2002: Republican House vote	52.9
2004: George W. Bush's vote	50.7
2004: Republican House vote	50.4

Table 6.1 Share of the vote in selected elections, 1996–2004

been put about by numerous commentators in a host of publications. Jill Lawrence, writing in *USA Today*, claimed that 'When George W. Bush took office [in 2001], half the country cheered and the other half seethed.' In its post-election edition in November 2000, *The Economist* claimed that 'the 50–50 nation appears to be made up of two big, separate voting blocks, with only a small number of swing voters in the middle.' In other words, America was deeply divided into two ideological camps and the traditional middle ground of the independent voter had well nigh disappeared.

If you want the full-throttle version of the culture war and 50–50 nation thesis, then try this from one-time Bill Clinton aide, Paul Begala, as quoted in the *Boston Herald* just 2 weeks after the 2000 election:

> You see the state where [African American] James Byrd was lynch-dragged behind a pickup truck until his body came apart — it's red. You see the state where Matthew Shepard was crucified on a split-rail fence for the crime of being gay — it's red. You see the state where right-wing extremists blew up a federal office building and murdered scores of federal employees — it's red...And the state where Bob Jones University spews its anti-Catholic bigotry — it's red too.

A number of people have rewritten the phrase from the Pledge of Allegiance about America being 'one nation, under God, indivisible'. *The Economist* (20 January 2001) described it as 'One Nation, Fairly Divisible, Under God'. Two years later, E. J. Dionne in the *Washington Post* saw America as 'one nation, deeply divided'. In 2004, Thomas Friedman viewed America as 'Two Nations Under God' (*New York Times*, 4 November 2004).

More shades of purple than red v blue

In *US Government & Politics 2006*, Chapter 2: 'Red and blue America', we pointed out that things are not quite that straightforward, hence the suggestion that America is more 'shades of purple' than red v blue. Whether it's 'red v blue', the 'culture war' or the '50–50 nation', the terminology is horribly oversimplified and the evidence brought to support it is certainly open to question.

West Virginia, a 'red state', has two Democratic (blue) senators. Its three-member state delegation in the House of Representatives includes two Democrats. It has a Democrat governor and Democrats control both houses of the state legislature. There are two 'blue states', Maine and New Hampshire, which are represented by two Republican senators. Massachusetts, Rhode Island and New York must be three of the 'bluest' states in the nation. In 2004, they gave John Kerry respectively 62%, 60% and 58% of the vote. Yet all three simultaneously had Republican governors. Connecticut, California, Maryland, Minnesota and Vermont are apparently five more deep red states. These five states, too, had Republican governors at the same time they were giving their votes to John Kerry.

Rick Warren, senior pastor of Saddleback Church in Orange County, California, puts it like this:

> There is no such thing as red state, blue state. If anything, it's red county, blue county. My state is not blue. It's all red except for the urban areas.

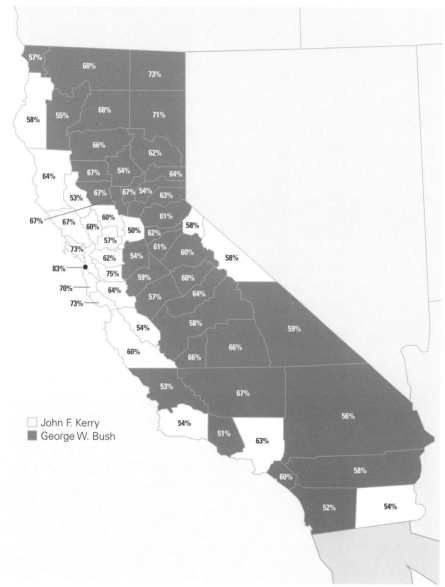

Figure 6.1 2004 presidential vote in California, by county

Figure 6.1 shows that Warren is right. Most of California in 2004 was Bush country, not Kerry country. Kerry's support was isolated around the urban areas — Eureka, San Francisco, Sacramento, Oakland, Santa Barbara, Los Angeles and San Diego.

Annual Survey, 2007

In his keynote speech at the 2004 Democratic National Convention, Barack Obama had this to say as a challenge to the conventional wisdom:

> We worship an awesome God in the blue states, and we don't like federal agents poking around our libraries in the red states. We coach little league in the blue states and, yes, we've got some gay friends in the red states.

Four myths about red v blue

In his recent book, *Culture War? The Myth of a Polarized America* (Pearson Longman, 2006), Morris Fiorina identifies four myths that he feels have contributed to the widely held views of America as a 50–50 nation.

Myth 1: America is a deeply divided nation

Many commentators on American politics have told us that the American electorate is polarised. We have already quoted *The Economist* as stating in November 2000 that American voters existed as 'two separate voting blocks, with only a small number of swing voters in the middle', reflecting the 'deep demographic divisions' in the nation. The presumption is that close elections must mean a polarised electorate. But Fiorina questions this assumption. He points out that there are two scenarios that might result in a close election. It could be, as is usually suggested, that the electorate is equally polarised, with half polarised to the left and half polarised to the right. But it could be that the electorate, while still mainly in the middle ground of politics, happens to be evenly divided. Fiorina suggests that America is not 'deeply divided', but 'closely divided'.

Take one hot-button issue: abortion. Fiorina finds that polling evidence shows that the majority of Americans take a moderate view on a woman's right to an abortion. They see abortion neither as an 'absolute right' nor as 'wrong under all circumstances'. Most Americans agree that a woman does have a right to choose, but that certain limits on that right are both prudent and right. A CBS News poll in 2003 — the thirtieth anniversary of the landmark Supreme Court case of *Roe v Wade* — found that 39% of Americans thought that abortion should be 'generally available', 38% thought it should be available but under stricter limits than at present, while only 22% thought it ought not to be permitted at all. Thus 77% of Americans agreed with a woman having a right to choose an abortion.

	Abortion should be generally available (%)	Abortion should be available, but with stricter limits than at present (%)	Abortion should not be available (%)
Democrats	43	35	21
Republicans	29	41	28
All	39	38	22

Source: www.cbsnews.com

Table 6.2 Americans' views of abortion, by party

When the responses are analysed, the picture is not one of a 'deeply divided' nation (see Table 6.2). While 28% of Republicans were completely against abortion, so were 21% of Democrats.

Looking at the same group of respondents by geographic region, Table 6.3 shows that there was not a huge difference from region to region. While 25% of southerners (red states) were against abortion, so were 19% in the northeast (blue states). Is this really a picture of a deeply divided country?

Region	Percentage against abortion
Northeast	19
Midwest	25
South	25
West	16

Source: www.cbsnews.com

Table 6.3 **Percentage of Americans against abortion, by region**

Myth 2: Believing that political activists are 'normal people'

Political activists are not 'normal people'. Normal people do not watch C-SPAN or rush home to catch *The News Hour with Jim Lehrer* on PBS. They don't belong to a political party. Most of them don't even vote. Howard Dean's much talked about e-mail list in the 2004 Democratic primaries had just 600,000 names on it — all doubtless political activists. Fiorina points out that this figure is only marginally greater than the number of admitted ferret owners in America!

The difference between political activists and normal people can most clearly be seen by comparing those who attend the respective quadrennial National Conventions as delegates with the general population. In August 2004, there was the regular *New York Times*/CBS News poll comparing the views of the Democratic and Republican National Convention delegates with those of ordinary voters. Here are five of the items from that poll:

1 Should the government do more to promote traditional values?

	Yes (%)	No (%)
All voters	40	57
2004 Democrat delegates	15	78
2004 Republican delegates	55	34

2 Should abortion be generally available, available under stricter limits or not permitted?

	Generally available (%)	Under stricter limits (%)	Not available (%)
All voters	34	40	24
Democrat voters	49	36	13
Republican voters	17	42	38
2004 Democrat delegates	75	17	2
2004 Republican delegates	13	39	38

Annual Survey, 2007

3 Should presidential candidates discuss the role of religion in their lives?

	Yes (%)	No (%)
All voters	48	50
2004 Democrat delegates	33	62
2004 Republican delegates	81	14

4 Are you a member of the National Rifle Association (NRA)?

	Yes (%)	No (%)
All voters	9	91
2004 Democrat delegates	2	98
2004 Republican delegates	24	75

5 Do you think of yourself as liberal, moderate or conservative?

	Liberal (%)	Moderate (%)	Conservative (%)
All voters	20	42	36
2004 Democrat delegates	41	52	3
2004 Republican delegates	1	33	63

One can see that on each of these five issues — traditional values, abortion, religion, NRA membership and ideology — the party activists were quite unrepresentative of ordinary people. On the question of abortion, one can see how different the delegates were, even from those who would normally vote for their respective parties. While there was a 32-point difference on the matter of abortion being generally available between Democrat and Republican *voters*, there was a 62-point difference between Democrat and Republican *delegates*.

Political activists are clearly not normal people; it follows that just because political activists are deeply divided, it is not the case that normal people are deeply divided.

Myth 3: The media give an accurate view of America

The trouble with most political journalists — and also, I suspect, many academics — is that they tend to spend most of their time talking to each other. They therefore come to believe that the world in which they live is normal, thinking that the views of those with whom they talk are the prevailing and representative views of the nation. In British politics, we are familiar with the concept of those who inhabit the 'Westminster village' — politicians, party activists and journalists. In American politics, the equivalent are those who live 'inside the Beltway' — Washington's version of the M25, which circles the city.

Journalists thrive on drama, hype, battles, wars and conflict. 'New survey shows Americans agree on most things — details at 11 o'clock' is not the kind of trailer likely to persuade people to stay up and watch the late evening news. Likewise, 'Democrats and Republicans similar on most issues' is not a headline that will sell newspapers. In 2004, the *Washington Post* ran a series of articles depicting the differences between red and blue America. One day there was a report from Sugar Land, Texas, featuring a man called Britton Stein:

> He lives in a house that has six guns in the closets and 21 crosses in the main hallway. He loves his family, hamburgers and his dog. He believes in God, prays daily and goes to church weekly. He drives a Chevy pickup truck. His beer is Bud Light. His saviour is Jesus Christ. His neighbours include Rep. Tom DeLay, the House majority [Republican] leader.

The next day, readers were introduced to Tom Harrison of San Francisco.

> Tom Harrison, 62, is a union official. Maryanne Harrison, 60, runs an after-school programme. Heather Harrison, 29, is a teacher. Matthew Harrison, 28, is an electrician. Their neighbourhood is filled with restaurants that are cafés, and stores that are boutiques, and their neighbours include straight people, gay people, rich people, homeless people, married people, single people and the House minority [Democrat] leader Rep. Nancy Pelosi.

Thus America is portrayed by the media not as a country of broad diversity but as one of deep division and difference.

Myth 4: Confusing 'positions' with 'choices'

Commentary states that because people's *choices* may be polarised, their *positions* are also polarised. In 2004, 89% of Democrats voted for John Kerry and 93% of Republicans voted for George W. Bush. Isn't that evidence of polarisation? But, states Fiorina, this is polarisation of people's choices, not polarisation of their positions.

Those who suggest that America is 'deeply divided' today might also suggest that the country is far more divided than it was back in the 1950s and 1960s — when Dwight Eisenhower and Richard Nixon were presidents, for example. But Republicans' support for George W. Bush in 2004 was about the same as it was for Eisenhower in 1952 and 1956 and for Richard Nixon in 1968 and 1972.

The significance of Bill Clinton and George W. Bush

It may be significant that for 16 years (1993–2009), America will have had two presidents who have been essentially divisive characters. There were those on the political right who spent the Clinton years (1993–2001) decrying the Democrat incumbent as a draft-dodging, pot-smoking, womanising liar. There have been those on the political left who have spent the Bush years (2001–09) calling the Republican incumbent a gun-toting, warmongering idiot. Presidents

have always been lampooned by their opponents, but the venom with which this has occurred in the last decade is, I would suggest, untypical. Presidents Gerald Ford, Jimmy Carter, Ronald Reagan and George H. W. Bush did not engender the same levels of sheer hate reserved for the two most recent occupants of the Oval Office.

It might be reasonable to suggest that the political temperature in America could cool significantly if the White House were to be occupied once more by someone of more temperate habits — a latter-day Dwight Eisenhower or Jimmy Carter.

Conclusions

The red v blue debate in American politics should be treated with a good deal of scepticism. It magnifies the differences and masks the similarities. Take the beliefs, perceptions and issues that are compared in Table 6.4. In terms of these 11 beliefs, perceptions and issues, the evidence shows that there is unsurprisingly little difference between red and blue states. The percentage point difference between the two is never greater then 12 and sometimes as small as 1. Little evidence here of a nation deeply divided into red and blue states.

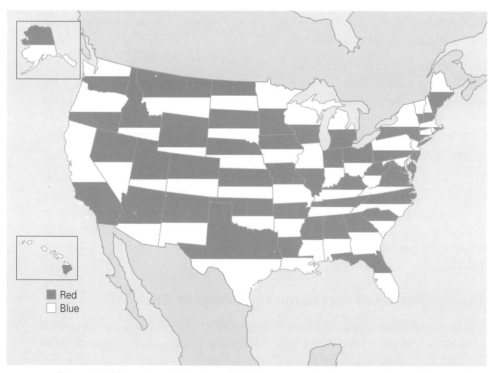

Figure 6.2 Map of the USA, showing states shaded by the proportion of the vote for Republican (red) and Democrat (blue) candidates, 2004

Belief/perception/issue	Red states (%)	Blue states (%)
Government is almost always wasteful	44	39
Discrimination keeps black people from getting ahead	21	25
Immigrants strengthen our country	32	44
You should fight for your country, whether it is right or wrong	43	35
Too much power is concentrated in large companies	62	64
Corporations make too much profit	43	44
Do whatever it takes to protect the environment	64	70
Religion is very important in my life	74	62
In favour of school vouchers	54	51
In favour of the death penalty	77	70
Belief in equality of women	82	83

Table 6.4 Beliefs, perceptions and issues: comparison of red and blue states (2000)

But most commentary on red v blue America perpetuates the idea that the country is deeply divided into oceans of red and islands of blue. It is not. Each state in America includes red and blue voters. Most, if not all, states in America have their Britton Steins and Tom Harrisons. America is not divided into tobacco-chewing, God-fearing, gun-loving rednecks in the red states and Volvo-driving, latte-drinking, godless, nose-pierced vegans in the blue states. This is a view popularised largely by ideological activists and sensationalistic news media. Next time you read red v blue, think purple.

Some of the material in this chapter is taken from Fiorina, M. P. (2006), *Culture War? The Myth of a Polarized America* (Pearson Longman).

Chapter 7

The 2006 mid-term congressional elections

> **What you need to know**
> - Mid-term congressional elections are those that come halfway through a president's 4-year term of office.
> - Therefore, they fall in years 1998, 2002, 2006, 2010 etc.
> - In these years there are elections for the whole of the House of Representatives and one third of the Senate.
> - The president's party may not always be the majority party in both houses of Congress.

The primaries

Year	House members defeated in primaries	Senators defeated in primaries
1986	2	0
1988	1	0
1990	1	0
1992	19	1
1994	4	0
1996	2	1
1998	1	0
2000	3	0
2002	8	1
2004	2	0
2006	2	1

Table 7.1 House and Senate incumbents defeated in primaries, 1986–2006

It is notoriously difficult to defeat incumbent House and Senate members in primaries. In the period between 1982 and 2004, only three Senators had been defeated in a primary, and one of those was a Senator who had been appointed to his Senate seat, rather than being elected. So it was a noteworthy event of the 2006 Senate primaries that an incumbent Senator was denied the nomination of his party. It was especially significant that this was a leading, long-standing member of the Senate — someone who just 6 years before had been his party's candidate for the vice-presidency: the Democrat Senator Joe Lieberman of Connecticut.

Lieberman was first elected to the US Senate in 1988 and was thus running for his fourth consecutive term. However, he had fallen out of favour with many Democrats for his wholehearted support of the war in Iraq and for the frequent remarks he had made in support of the actions of Republican President George W. Bush. Lieberman was challenged in the Democratic Senate primary by the businessman Ned Lamont, whose website (**www.nedlamont.com**) stated that 'like most Connecticut Democrats, and most Americans, I am tired of being represented by a senator who is not willing to stand up to the President'. On 8 August 2006 Lamont defeated Lieberman by 52% to 48% and thus became the official Democratic candidate. Lieberman immediately announced that he would contest the seat as an Independent.

The other Senator who was thought to be in real danger in the primaries was Rhode Island Republican Senator Lincoln Chafee, the most liberal Republican in the chamber. Conservative Republicans in Rhode Island referred to Chafee as being a 'RINO' — a Republican In Name Only. But Chafee fought off the strong challenge from conservative Cranston Mayor Steve Laffey by 54% to 46%.

In the House of Representatives, Democrat Cynthia McKinney (Georgia) lost a primary for the second time in 4 years. McKinney, an African-American, had been defeated in the primary in 2002 after suggesting that President Bush may have known in advance about the attacks on New York and Washington on 11 September 2001. She gained her seat back in 2004. In 2006 she lost again in the primary after a much-publicised incident in which she punched a (white) Capitol Hill police officer and then accused him of 'racial profiling' and 'inappropriate touching'.

The only other incumbent to lose in the House primaries was one-term moderate Republican Joe Schwarz in Michigan's 7th Congressional District. Schwarz had struggled to gain the Republican nomination in 2004, when he received just 24% of the vote in a six-way primary. This time around he was defeated by former state representative Tim Walberg, by 53% to 47%. Walberg had the backing of conservative political action committees such as Right to Life and the Club for Growth, while Schwarz was backed by Senator John McCain of Arizona and President Bush. So much for White House influence.

The Senate results

At the end of the 109th Congress, the Republicans held 55 seats in the Senate and the Democrats 44, and there was one independent — James Jeffords of Vermont, who caucused and usually voted with the Democrats. Thus the Democrats needed to make an overall gain of six seats in order to win back control of the Senate, which they had lost in the last mid-term elections in 2002. Their task looked rather difficult. Of the 33 seats being contested in 2006, only 15 were Republican-held, and only six or seven of them looked winnable. The Democrats also had one or two vulnerable seats of their own,

notably in New Jersey and Florida. To win control of the Senate, the Democrats would have to win virtually every Republican marginal seat while holding on to all of their own. It seemed a tall order, and few pundits thought it would happen, but happen it did. When the results were finally in, the Democrats had gained six seats and lost none, giving them a 51–49 seat edge over the Republicans (see Table 7.2).

Six incumbent Senators were defeated on election day, all of them Republicans, the highest figure since 1986 (see Table 7.3). The Republicans suffered their heaviest defeats in the Northeast and Mid-Atlantic seats, with Pennsylvania, Ohio and Rhode Island falling to the Democrats. The defeats of Rick Santorum in Pennsylvania and Lincoln Chafee in Rhode Island showed that while being an ardent Bush-supporter (Santorum) proved a liability, distancing oneself from the President (Chafee) was no protection either.

In Ohio, the moderately conservative Mike DeWine lost to the member of the House of Representatives who most frequently opposed the stated position of President Bush, Congressman Sherrod Brown. In Missouri, Jim Talent was swept out of office after just 4 years, defeated by former state legislator and city prosecutor Claire McCaskill. Conrad Burns lost in Montana following his links to the disgraced lobbyist Jack Abramoff. The biggest surprise of all was the defeat of George Allen in Virginia. Allen had begun the election cycle hoping to use his re-election as a launch pad for a presidential bid in 2008. He ended it losing in the closest of races — by just under 9,000 votes out of a total of 2.3 million. Allen's biggest gaffe during the election was in making a racist slur against a black staff member of his Democrat opponent, Jim Webb.

The one race the Democrats had in their sights that they did not win was the open seat in Tennessee, caused by the retirement of the Senate Majority Leader Bill Frist. The former Mayor of Chattanooga, Bob Corker, managed to swim against the Democrat tide. He held the seat by a 3-percentage point margin against a strong challenge from the Democrat Congressman Harold Ford. Ford would have become the first African-American elected to the Senate from the south since the Civil War.

The Democrats suffered more of an embarrassment than a disappointment in Connecticut, where their official candidate Ned Lamont failed to unseat Joe Lieberman, who he had defeated in the Democratic primary earlier in the year. Lieberman, standing on the 'Connecticut for Lieberman' ticket, won with votes from Democrats, Independents and large numbers of Republicans. The Republican candidate, Alan Schlesinger, came home with just 9.7% of the vote. Clearly many Republicans in Connecticut, seeing Lieberman's support for the President's policy in Iraq, decided to give him their vote and thereby embarrass the Democrats. Lieberman will continue to sit as a Democrat in the new Congress.

State	Winner	Party	%	Opponent	Party	%
Arizona	**Jon Kyl**	R	53	Jim Pederson	D	44
California	**Dianne Feinstein**	D	60	Dick Mountjoy	R	35
Connecticut	**Joe Lieberman**	Ind	50	Ned Lamont	D	40
				Alan Schlesinger	R	10
Delaware	**Thomas Carper**	D	70	Jan Ting	R	29
Florida	**Bill Nelson**	D	60	Katherine Harris	R	38
Hawaii	**Daniel Akaka**	D	61	Cynthia Thielen	R	37
Indiana	**Richard Lugar**	R	87	Steve Osborn	Lib	13
Maine	**Olympia Snowe**	R	74	Jean Hay Bright	D	20
Maryland	Benjamin Cardin	D	55	Michael Steele	R	44
Massachusetts	**Edward Kennedy**	D	69	Ken Chase	R	31
Michigan	**Debbie Stabenow**	D	57	Mike Bouchard	R	41
Minnesota	Amy Klobuchar	D	58	Mark Kennedy	R	38
Mississippi	**Trent Lott**	R	64	Erik Fleming	D	35
Missouri	Claire McCaskill	D	49	**Jim Talent**	R	47
Montana	Jon Tester	D	49	**Conrad Burns**	R	48
Nebraska	**Ben Nelson**	D	64	Pete Ricketts	R	36
Nevada	**John Ensign**	R	55	Jack Carter	D	41
New Jersey	**Bob Menendez**	D	53	Tom Kean	R	45
New Mexico	**Jeff Bingaman**	D	70	Allen McCulloch	R	29
New York	**Hillary Clinton**	D	67	John Spencer	R	31
North Dakota	**Kent Conrad**	D	69	Dwight Grotberg	R	30
Ohio	Sherrod Brown	D	56	**Mike DeWine**	R	44
Pennsylvania	Bob Casey	D	59	**Rick Santorum**	R	41
Rhode Island	Sheldon Whitehouse	D	53	**Lincoln Chafee**	R	47
Tennessee	Bob Corker	R	51	Harold Ford	D	48
Texas	**Kay Bailey Hutchison**	R	62	Barbara Radnofsky	D	36
Utah	**Orrin Hatch**	R	63	Pete Ashdown	D	31
Vermont	Bernie Sanders	Ind	66	Rich Tarrant	R	32
Virginia	Jim Webb	D	49	**George Allen**	R	49
Washington	**Maria Cantwell**	D	58	Mike McGavick	R	40
West Virginia	**Robert Byrd**	D	64	John Raese	R	34
Wisconsin	**Herb Kohl**	D	67	Robert Lorge	R	30
Wyoming	**Craig Thomas**	R	70	Dale Groutage	D	30

Lib: Libertarian Party

Table 7.2 Results of Senate elections, 2006 (incumbents in bold)

In New York, Hillary Clinton romped home with 67% of the vote, a significant increase on her 55% in 2000. But even Clinton reached nowhere near the levels of acclaim enjoyed by Republican Richard Lugar in Indiana. He was elected to his sixth term with a whopping 87% of the vote. The Democrats were so sure of his re-election that they didn't even bother to oppose him. Democrat Robert Byrd of West Virginia entered the record books by being re-elected to his ninth term. Byrd, who will turn 90 in November 2007, entered the Senate in 1958 and has served under ten presidents.

Of the ten new Senators elected in 2006, three are former members of Congress: Sherrod Brown of Ohio, Benjamin Cardin of Maryland and Bernie Sanders of Vermont. Two more women were elected to the Senate in these mid-term elections, both Democrats: Amy Klobuchar of Minnesota and Claire McCaskill of Missouri. This brings the number of women in the Senate to an all-time high of 16 — 11 Democrats and five Republicans. Two prominent African-Americans ran for the Senate — Michael Steele for the Republicans in Maryland and Harold Ford for the Democrats in Tennessee — but both lost, leaving the number of African-Americans in the Senate unchanged at one.

Table 7.3 shows that the re-election rate in the Senate, at 79.3%, was the lowest since 1986. With four retirees and six incumbents defeated, there will be ten new Senators in the 110th Congress. Perhaps the most extraordinary statistic of the mid-term elections for the Senate is that the Republicans won only nine of the 33 races. That statistic in itself shows how difficult Republican candidates found things in this election cycle.

Year	Retired	Sought re-election	Defeated in primary	Defeated in general election	Total re-elected	Percentage re-elected who sought re-election
1986	6	28	0	7	21	75.0
1988	6	27	0	4	23	85.2
1990	3	32	0	1	31	96.9
1992	7	28	1	4	23	82.1
1994	9	26	0	2	24	92.3
1996	13	21	1	1	19	90.5
1998	5	29	0	3	26	89.6
2000	5	29	0	5	24	82.8
2002	5	28	1	3	24	85.7
2004	8	26	0	1	25	96.1
2006	4	29	1*	6	23	79.3

* Senator Joe Lieberman (D-Connecticut) was defeated in the Democratic primary but was then re-elected as an Independent and will sit as a Democrat

Table 7.3 Senators retired, defeated and re-elected, 1986–2006

The House results

At the end of the 109th Congress, ignoring vacant seats, the Republicans held 232 seats, the Democrats 202, with one Independent — Bernie Sanders of Vermont, who caucuses with the Democrats. The Democrats therefore needed to make an overall gain of 15 seats to win back control of the House of Representatives, which they lost in the mid-term elections of 1994. By the late summer of election year, it looked increasingly likely that they would achieve this. And as the bad news from Iraq rolled in, the President's approval rating continued to decline and the Republican-related scandals mounted up, which made their task look progressively easier. In the end, the Democrats won 29 seats from the Republicans, plus the seat in Vermont vacated by Bernie Sanders, to give them an overall gain of 30 seats. Thus the final party balance was reversed to be 232 Democrats and 203 Republicans (At the time of going to press, the result in Florida's 13th congressional district was still uncertain. These figures presume that the Republicans will hold the seat.) This ended 12 years of Republican control of the House, the longest stretch of time since the period between the elections of 1920 and 1932.

Altogether, 21 Republican incumbents were defeated on election day, the highest number since 1996. This gave a re-election rate of 94.3%, a 10-year low (see Table 7.4). The list of defeated incumbents (Table 7.5) includes both recently elected members and those with some level of seniority. Five of those defeated were members of the 'Class of 1994', who had arrived in Washington that year as part of the new Republican majority. Charles Bass of New Hampshire, Gil Gutknecht of Minnesota, J. D. Hayworth of Arizona, John Hostettler of Indiana and Sue Kelly of New York arrived with the Republican majority and left as the majority was conceded back to the Democrats.

Year	Retired	Sought re-election	Defeated in primary	Defeated in general election	Total re-elected	Percentage re-elected who sought re-election
1986	38	393	2	6	385	98.0
1988	26	409	1	6	402	98.3
1990	27	407	1	15	391	96.1
1992	67	368	19	24	325	88.3
1994	48	387	4	34	349	90.2
1996	50	383	2	21	360	94.0
1998	33	401	1	6	394	98.3
2000	32	403	3	6	394	97.8
2002	38	397	8	8	381	96.0
2004	29	404	2	7	395	97.8
2006	28	405	2	21	382	94.3

Table 7.4 House members retired, defeated and re-elected, 1986–2006

House member	Party	Congressional District	First elected
Charles Bass	Republican	New Hampshire 2	1994
Jeb Bradley	Republican	New Hampshire 1	2002
Chris Chocola	Republican	Indiana 2	2002
Mike Fitzpatrick	Republican	Pennsylvania 8	2004
Gil Gutknecht	Republican	Minnesota 1	1994
Melissa Hart	Republican	Pennsylvania 4	2000
J. D. Hayworth	Republican	Arizona 5	1994
John Hostettler	Republican	Indiana 8	1994
Nancy Johnson	Republican	Connecticut 5	1982
Sue Kelly	Republican	New York 19	1994
Jim Leach	Republican	Iowa 2	1976
Anne Northrop	Republican	Kentucky 3	1996
Richard Pombo	Republican	California 11	1992
Jim Ryun	Republican	Kansas 2	1996
Clay Shaw	Republican	Florida 22	1980
Don Sherwood	Republican	Pennsylvania 10	1998
Rob Simmons	Republican	Connecticut 2	2000
Mike Sodrel	Republican	Indiana 9	2004
John Sweeney	Republican	New York 20	1998
Charles Taylor	Republican	North Carolina 11	1990
Curt Weldon	Republican	Pennsylvania 7	1986

Table 7.5 House incumbents defeated in the general election, 2006

The list shown in Table 7.5 includes one former and one serving standing committee chairman. Jim Leach lost his bid for a sixteenth term in Congress. Leach was first elected to the House in 1976. He had been chairman of the House Banking and Financial Services Committee between 1995 and 2001. Also defeated was Richard Pombo of California, the serving chairman of the House Resources Committee. Both had won re-election easily just 2 years before.

The geographic distribution of Republican losses was significant (see Table 7.6). Of the 29 seats that the Republicans lost, 12 (41%) were in the Northeast, making the region even more blue than it was before. Republicans lost four seats in Pennsylvania, three in New York, two in both Connecticut and New Hampshire, and one in Ohio. They also lost nine seats in the Midwest (including three in Indiana), five in the South and three in the West. In 2006 the Republicans lost ten of the 18 House Districts which, in 2004, elected a Republican House member but voted for Democrat John Kerry for president.

Region	Districts lost by Republicans
Northeast: 12	Connecticut 2
	Connecticut 5
	New Hampshire 1
	New Hampshire 2
	New York 19
	New York 20
	New York 24
	Ohio 18
	Pennsylvania 4
	Pennsylvania 7
	Pennsylvania 8
	Pennsylvania 10
South: 5	Florida 16
	Florida 22
	Kentucky 3
	North Carolina 11
	Texas 22
Midwest: 9	Colorado 7
	Indiana 2
	Indiana 8
	Indiana 9
	Iowa 1
	Iowa 2
	Kansas 2
	Minnesota 1
	Wisconsin 8
West: 3	Arizona 5
	Arizona 8
	California 11

Table 7.6 Republican losses in the House by geographic region

Of the 16 House members who retired to seek other elective offices (Table 7.7 overleaf), three were elected to the Senate and three were elected as state Governor. The other ten lost their bids either in the primary or the general election.

In terms of the gender make-up of the House, six women left the House at the end of the 109th Congress: five defeated at re-election and Katherine

Harris, who made an unsuccessful bid for the Senate seat in Florida. However, ten new women members will join the 110th Congress — eight Democrats and two Republicans — bringing the total number of women in the House to a new record high of 71 (51 Democrats and 20 Republicans). The racial mix of the new Congress will include 40 African-Americans and 23 Hispanics; neither figure is changed from the end of the previous Congress. As a result of the 2006 elections, the House has a Buddhist member, Mazie Hirono of Hawaii, and a Muslim, Keith Ellison of Minnesota — both Democrats.

House member	Party	State/Congressional Disctrict	Running for...	Result
Bob Beauprez	R	Colorado 7	Governor	Lost
Sherrod Brown	D	Ohio 13	Senate	Elected to Senate
Benjamin Cardin	D	Maryland 3	Senate	Elected to Senate
Ed Case	D	Hawaii 2	Senate	Lost in primary
Jim Davis	D	Florida 11	Governor	Lost
Harold Ford	D	Tennessee 9	Senate	Lost
Jim Gibbons	R	Nevada 2	Governor	Elected Governor
Mark Green	R	Wisconsin 8	Governor	Lost
Katherine Harris	R	Florida 13	Senate	Lost
Ernest Istook	R	Oklahoma 5	Governor	Lost
Mark Kennedy	R	Minnesota 6	Senate	Lost
Jim Nussle	R	Iowa 1	Governor	Lost
Tom Osborne	R	Nebraska 3	Governor	Lost in primary
Butch Otter	R	Idaho 1	Governor	Elected Governor
Bernie Sanders	I	Vermont AL	Senate	Elected to Senate
Ted Strickland	D	Ohio 6	Governor	Elected Governor

Table 7.7 House members seeking other elective offices, 2006

The results overall

When the final counts and run-offs were completed, the Republicans had overall losses of six seats in the Senate and 29 seats in the House. In comparison to previous mid-term losses for the president's party, these were quite modest. The Republicans managed to avoid the scale of losses sustained by the Democrats in 1994 or of the Republicans 6 years into Eisenhower's presidency in 1958.

In Table 7.8, there are six sets of elections (shown in bold) that were held 6 years into a president's term of office: 1918 (Wilson), 1938 (Roosevelt), 1958

(Eisenhower), 1986 (Reagan), 1998 (Clinton) and 2006 (George W. Bush). The average losses for these elections are 28 seats in the House and just under seven seats in the Senate. In other words, the losses sustained by the Republicans in 2006 were par for the course for a president 6 years into his term of office. It could have been a lot worse. There were 20 House seats that Republican candidates won with 51% or less of the popular vote — districts like those of Heather Wilson in New Mexico or Barbara Cubin in Wyoming. If those 20 seats had also fallen to the Democrats, then the Republicans would have been looking at losses on a par with what the Democrats suffered in the so-called 'Republican Revolution' of 1994.

Year	Party holding presidency	Gains/losses for president's party in: House	Senate
1914	D	59	+5
1918	**D**	**−19**	**−6**
1922	R	−75	−8
1926	R	−10	−6
1930	R	−49	−8
1934	D	+9	+10
1938	**D**	**−71**	**−6**
1942	D	−55	−9
1946	D	−45	−12
1950	D	−29	−6
1954	R	−18	−1
1958	**R**	**−48**	**−13**
1962	D	−4	+3
1966	D	−47	−4
1970	R	−12	+2
1974	R	−48	−5
1978	D	−15	−5
1982	R	−26	+1
1986	**R**	**−5**	**−8**
1990	R	−8	−1
1994	D	−52	−8
1998	**D**	**+5**	**0**
2002	R	+5	+2
2006	**R**	**−29**	**−6**

Table 7.8 Losses by the president's party in mid-term elections, 1914–2006

Annual Survey, 2007

Who voted for whom, and why?

Category (percentage of population)	Republican vote 2004 (%)	Republican vote 2006 (%)	Change in Republican vote (%)
Men (49)	55	47	−8
Women (51)	48	43	−5
White (79)	58	51	−7
African-American (10)	11	10	−1
Hispanic (8)	43	30	−13
White men (39)	61	53	−8
White women (40)	55	50	−5
Aged 18–29 (21)	45	38	−7
Aged 30–44 (24)	53	45	−8
Aged 45–59 (34)	51	46	−5
Aged 60+ (29)	54	48	−6
All Protestant (55)	59	54	−5
White Protestant (44)	67	61	−6
Catholic (26)	52	44	−8
Jewish (2)	25	12	−13
Democrats (38)	11	7	−4
Republicans (36)	93	91	−2
Independents (26)	48	39	−9
Liberal (20)	13	11	−2
Moderate (47)	45	38	−7
Conservative (32)	84	78	−6
Family income:			
Under $15,000 (7)	36	30	−6
$15–30,000 (12)	42	36	−6
$30–50,000 (21)	49	43	−6
$50–75,000 (22)	56	48	−8
$75–100,000 (16)	55	47	−8
Over $100,000 (23)	58	51	−7
Church attendance:			
More than weekly (17)	64	60	−4
Weekly (28)	58	53	−5
Monthly (12)	50	41	−9
A few times a year (25)	45	38	−7
Never (15)	36	30	−6

Category (percentage of population)	Republican vote 2004 (%)	Republican vote 2006 (%)	Change in Republican vote (%)
Region:			
North-east (22)	43	35	–8
Midwest (27)	51	47	–4
South (30)	58	53	–5
West (21)	49	43	–6
2004 voters:			
Kerry (43)	–	7	–
Bush (49)	–	83	–
Others (4)	–	23	–
Didn't vote (4)	–	32	–

Source: www.cnn.com

Table 7.9 Who voted for whom: comparison of 2004 and 2006

The national exit poll data from the House elections (summarised in Table 7.9) show how support for the Republican Party has slumped in the 2 years since George W. Bush was re-elected. In every category in this table, Republican support has fallen by between 1 and 13 percentage points.

The most significant decline in support was among Hispanic voters, where Republican support fell from 43% in 2004 to just 30% in 2006. Such a significant decline in the Hispanic vote matters because — at more than 14 million — they are now the nation's largest ethnic minority. The reason for this decline was undoubtedly the Republicans' position on immigration reform. Those tough-talking campaign ads by conservative Republican candidates may not have had the desired effect. President Bush's reaction to the loss of Hispanic voters was to choose Cuban American Senator Mel Martinez of Florida to take over as chairman of the Republican National Committee from January 2007. 'A lot of Republican candidates chose immigration as the wedge issue, and polls seem to bear out that it was an error for them to do that,' commented Reverend Luis Cortés, founder of Esperanza USA, a network of Latino Christian groups. 'I think Mel Martinez is a perfect person to help [Hispanics] find their way back [to the Republican Party],' he added.

It wasn't only Hispanics who walked away from the Republican Party. Support among both males and Catholics was down 8 percentage points. Republicans lost support among every age group and region. Decline was greatest in the Northeast, where they lost 8 percentage points and consequently suffered the heaviest losses in terms of seats. Support among Independents, who had given the Republicans 48% of their votes in 2004,

was down by 9 percentage points. The Republicans lost these elections, despite the fact that 49% of the voters were Bush voters in 2004 and only 43% voted for Kerry in that year. Frequency of church attendance continued to have a high correlation with voting Republicans, but the Republicans still lost an election in which 45% of voters told pollsters that they attended church either weekly or more often.

In 2004, 20 of the groups detailed in Table 7.9 had given the majority of their support to the Republicans. By 2006, this number was down to 11 groups. Among the nine groups lost were men, those over 30, Catholics and people living in the Midwest.

Exit poll data also showed a correlation between voters' opinions of President Bush and the war in Iraq and the way they cast their votes. The overwhelming majority (84%) of those voters who approved of the President's handling of his job voted Republican. The trouble for the Republicans was that they represented a minority of voters (see Table 7.10). The vast majority (81%) of those who approved of the US war in Iraq voted Republican, but again, they were a minority of voters. The Republicans polled 79% of those who thought the country was going in the right direction, but only 41% of voters overall agreed, and 55% thought it was heading in the wrong direction. When voters were asked whether they voted on local or national issues, once again the Democrats' success was clear. The Democrats had spent the entire campaign trying to 'nationalise' these mid-term elections — to turn them into a referendum on President Bush. They succeeded. Sixty percent of voters said they voted on national issues, with only 34% voting on local issues.

Issue (%)	Democrat (%)	Republican (%)
How Bush is handling his job:		
Approve (43)	14	84
Disapprove (57)	82	16
US war in Iraq:		
Approve (42)	18	81
Disapprove (56)	80	18
Country going in the right direction:		
Yes (41)	20	79
No (55)	78	20
Which mattered more:		
Local issues (34)	51	47
National issues (60)	54	45

Table 7.10 Voting determinants: exit poll figures on why people voted in House races in 2006

Why did the Democrats win?

Usually mid-term elections are about local issues. Occasionally, national issues prevail. They did in 1994 when the Republicans swept to power in both Houses on the back of their Contract with America. And, as we have seen from the exit poll data, national issues also prevailed in 2006 and swept the Democrats back into power in both Houses. But why did the Democrats win? There are three major factors worth analysing.

(i) Republican incompetence

The Republicans lost control of Congress because they were perceived as being incompetent. A majority of voters held this view, both of the Republican president and the Republican Congress. Just as George W. Bush's high approval ratings had helped congressional candidates to win seats in both Houses in the mid-term elections of 2002, so Bush's low approval ratings caused congressional candidates to lose seats in both Houses in 2006. No matter how far Republican candidates (such as Senator Lincoln Chafee of Rhode Island) distanced themselves from the President, they could not escape the voters' ire.

Table 7.11 shows the high degree of correlation between the president's party winning or losing seats in the House of Representatives and the president's approval rating. Look at the record of presidents Ronald Reagan, Bill Clinton and George W. Bush in each of their two sets of mid-term elections. When their approval ratings are high — respectively in 1986, 1998 and 2002 — their parties do well in the mid-term House races. When their approval ratings are low —1982, 1994 and 2006 — their parties do badly. With George W. Bush's approval ratings languishing throughout 2006, the Republicans were always likely to have a torrid time in the mid-term elections.

Year	President	Approval rating	House seats won/lost by president's party
1998	Bill Clinton (D)	66%	+5
2002	George W. Bush (R)	63%	+5
1986	Ronald Reagan (R)	63%	−5
1990	George Bush (R)	58%	−8
1970	Richard Nixon (R)	57%	−12
1978	Jimmy Carter (D)	49%	−15
1974	Gerald Ford (R)	47%	−48
1994	Bill Clinton (D)	46%	−52
1982	Ronald Reagan (R)	43%	−26
2006	George W. Bush (R)	39%	−29

Table 7.11 Presidents' approval ratings and gains/losses by their party in House mid-term elections, 1970–2006

For many voters, there were a whole raft of issues, events and crises, and it was the President's handling of these that led them to question his competence and say they 'disapproved' rather than 'approved' of the way he was doing his job. The failure to plan for a post-Saddam Iraq was one. This merged into a second for many voters: the Bush administration's perceived incompetence in the conduct of the Iraq war (we shall return to this point later). Then there was the federal government's response to Hurricane Katrina in 2005. And for conservative voters, there was the fiasco of the President's nomination of Harriet Miers to the Supreme Court, where he was forced to withdraw that nomination in the face of fierce opposition from conservatives. The President's failure to veto big-spending bills and to increase the spending of the federal government only further annoyed the Republican base.

This was compounded by voters' views of the Republican-controlled Congress. Congress's approval rating was a good 10 percentage points below that of the President. When voters were asked throughout the campaign whether they were more likely to vote for a Democrat or Republican candidate, the Democrats usually held a double-digit lead. Congress — and the President — were blamed for failure to deliver on a number of major policy issues, such as immigration reform and social security reform.

(ii) Republican scandals

Voters can forgive a bit of scandal. But when it comes in cartloads — as it did for the Republican Congress — then voters are less forgiving. In the year between September 2005 and September 2006, the Republicans managed to attract the following negative publicity concerning scandals:

- 'DeLay Indicted in Texas Finance Probe', proclaimed the front-page headline of the *Washington Post* on 29 September 2005. The story began:

  > A Texas grand jury indicted House Majority Leader Tom DeLay (R-Texas) yesterday on a charge of criminally conspiring with two political associates to inject illegal corporate contributions into 2002 state elections that helped the Republican Party reorder the congressional map in Texas and cement its control of the House of Representatives in Washington. The indictment forced DeLay, one of the Republicans' most powerful leaders and fundraisers, to step aside under House rules barring such posts to those accused of criminal conduct.

  Eventually, DeLay resigned from Congress, but it was too late for Republicans to replace his name on the November 2006 ballot. His would-be Republican replacement, Shelley Sekula Gibbs, had to get supporters to write her name in on the ballot paper. She lost to Democrat Nick Lampson by 10 percentage points.

- Two months later, on 28 November, another Republican congressman, Randy 'Duke' Cunningham of California, resigned his House seat after pleading guilty to conspiracy, tax evasion and bribery charges.

- On 3 January 2006, Lobbyist Jack Abramoff pled guilty to fraud, tax evasion and conspiracy charges. Abramoff had links to a number of Republican members of Congress. Here's how the *National Journal* reported the mid-term electoral fall-out for one such member, Congressman Richard Pombo of California:

  > Two years ago, Republican Richard Pombo carried California's 11th Congressional District against Democrat Jerry McNerney by 61 percent to 39 percent. Since then, as the Republican who took more Jack Abramoff money than any other California member, Pombo has been beset by ethics allegations. On Tuesday [7 November 2006], Pombo lost to McNerney, 53 percent to 47 percent, despite outspending him by more than 2-to-1.

  The Abramoff link had caused a swing of 28 points against the Republican congressman.

- On 15 September 2006 another Republican House member, Bob Ney of Ohio, pleaded guilty to two counts of conspiracy and false statements relating to the Abramoff investigation. Bob Ney was chairman of the House Administration Committee and had been re-elected to a sixth term in 2004, with 66% of the votes in Ohio's 18th Congressional District. In 2006, the Democrat candidate Zack Space — a political novice — won the District with 61% of the vote.

  Republican Senator Conrad Burns of Montana was another Abramoff casualty, losing a close race to Democrat Jon Tester by less than 1 percentage point.

- On 29 September 2006 Republican Congressman Mark Foley of Florida resigned after the disclosure that he had sent explicit e-mails to a school-age boy working as a Page in the House of Representatives. In 2004, Foley had been re-elected to his sixth term in Florida's 16th Congressional District with 68% of the vote. With Foley's name still on the ballot paper, the Republican candidate Joe Negron lost to Democrat Tim Mahoney by less than 2 percentage points.

- To cap it all, there was another Republican House member — John Sweeney of New York — who showed up worse the wear for drink at a campaign event and then got into a fracas with his wife, who ended up calling the police. Sweeney saw his share of the vote in his New York District fall from a winning 66% in 2004 to losing 46% in 2006.

- Time for one more? How about Pennsylvania Republican House member Don Sherwood, who was accused of trying to choke his mistress in his Washington apartment during an extra-marital affair in 2005? In 2004, Sherwood was re-elected with a whopping 94% of the vote against only minor party opposition. Just 2 years later he lost with a mere 47% of the vote.

Put these issues together — incompetence and infidelity — and you can see why there were so many angry voters in 2006. As is often the case in voting, anger is often a better motivator than affection. In exit polls, 74% of voters said 'corruption' was important in their decision.

Chapter 7

(iii) Bush's war

In the only televised debate of 1980, Governor Ronald Reagan famously floored his opponent President Jimmy Carter by posing the question to the viewers: 'Are you better off than you were 4 years ago?' But few remember the equally powerful follow-up question: 'Is America as respected throughout the world as it was?' If the Republicans in 2006 had posed the first of Reagan's questions, they might have got a 'yes' from the majority of voters. But if they posed the second, they would certainly have got a 'no'.

By now, the majority of Americans disapproved of America's war in Iraq. Immediately after the attacks on New York and Washington in September 2001, America was enveloped in a tide of friendship. The day after the bombings, the French newspaper *Le Monde* had the headline: 'We are all Americans now'. But in the eyes of many Americans, the administration of George W. Bush was guilty of squandering this goodwill with its ill-conceived invasion of Iraq.

Iraq mattered in the mid-term elections of 2006. Two-thirds of voters said the war was important to them. Such voters favoured Democrats decisively. Writing in the post-election edition of the *National Journal*, Carl Cannon put it this way: 'Bush hadn't lost an election since 1978, but he lost this one on Tuesday, and Iraq was the main reason'. John McIntyre on the Real Clear Politics website (**www.realclearpolitics.com**) had this to say:

> Make no mistake about it, the driving issue in this election was Iraq. Heading into Election Day the big unknown was how the public would speak on the issue of the war. It was clear before the election that there was a growing realisation in the country that Iraq was not going well, that it was a mess and a significant problem. However, it was unclear whether that frustration would be enough of a catalyst to get the voters who chose to go to the polls to side with the Democrats over the Republicans. The answer was clear that it was.

Veteran political commentator Robert Novak concluded that 'opposition to the war and the President produced a virulent anti-Republican mood'.

Regime change on Capitol Hill

When Congress reassembled at the beginning of January 2007 for the start of the 110th Congress, every leadership post and every committee chairmanship had changed — the first time this had occurred in 12 years.

In the Senate, the Democrats confirmed **Harry Reid** of Nevada as Majority Leader and **Richard Durbin** of Illinois as Majority Whip. They had held the parallel minority posts in the previous Congress. The Senate Republicans had to pick a new leadership team following the retirement of Bill Frist of Tennessee, who was the Republican leader in the previous Congress. Elected without opposition as Republican (Minority) Leader was **Mitch McConnell** of Kentucky, the former Republican Whip. The big surprise was the election of

Senator **Trent Lott** of Mississippi as Minority Whip. Lott defeated Lamar Alexander of Tennessee by 25 votes to 24 among Republican Senators. He had been forced to step down as the Senate Majority Leader following the 2002 mid-term elections, after he had suggested that the country would have been better off if the then-segregationist Strom Thurmond of South Carolina had been elected president in 1948 rather than Harry Truman.

In the House, the Democrats confirmed **Nancy Pelosi** of California as Speaker, the first time in the history of Congress that a woman had held the top leadership position. But Speaker-elect Pelosi immediately ran into a political storm of her own making. On the weekend before House Democrats were due to pick their new leadership team, Pelosi made a public endorsement of John Murtha of Pennsylvania for the post of House Majority Leader, in preference to the front-runner, **Steny Hoyer** of Maryland. In the ensuing vote, Hoyer was chosen by 149 votes to 86. It was a stunning rebuke to Pelosi in her first public decision after the election. Murtha had received much media attention following his call for the withdrawal of American troops from Iraq. But most House Democrats regarded Hoyer as the safer pair of hands, someone of consummate political skill. 'He's very, very effective,' commented Jerrold Nadler of New York. The House Democrats then chose **James Clyburn**, an African-American from South Carolina, as House Majority Whip.

House Republicans elected their top two leaders by big majorities: **John Boehner** of Ohio as Minority Leader (168–27 over Mike Pence of Indiana) and **Roy Blunt** of Missouri as Minority Whip (137–57 over John Shadegg of Arizona).

Regime change took place in the committee rooms of Congress too. The seniority rule largely held as the Democrats with the longest continuous service on each committee were generally confirmed as chairman. In the Senate, women now chair two of the standing committees: Environment and Public Works by Barbara Boxer and Rules and Administration by Dianne Feinstein. Both are Senators from California.

What strikes one about these committee chairmen is their age. Only Kent Conrad (Budget) is under 60; three are in their seventies and a further three in their eighties — Daniel Inouye and Daniel Akaka are both 82 and Robert Byrd is 89. It's not much better in the House, with the list of standing committee chairmen including Charles Rangel (76), John Conyers (77), Louise Slaughter (77), Tom Lantos (78) and John Dingell (80).

Some committees will see a significant ideological shift as a result of the switch from Republican to Democrat chairmen. Take the Senate Foreign Relations Committee, for example, where conservative Republican Richard Lugar of Indiana gives way to liberal Democrat Joseph Biden of Delaware.

Not only will the new House have an African-American as Majority Whip, but five other African-Americans are in line for House committee chairmanships:

John Conyers of Michigan (Judiciary); Charles Rangel of New York (Ways and Means); Bennie Thompson of Mississippi (Homeland Security); Juanita Millender-McDonald of California (House Administration); and Alcee Hastings of Florida (Intelligence). Certainly the new Congress looks very different from its predecessor.

Likely effects

There is some evidence that the checks and balances between the president and Congress are more effective when the White House and Capitol Hill are controlled by different parties. 'Divided government' — as we call such an arrangement — often leads to more effective monitoring of the executive by the legislature. In the 40-year period between 1969 and 2009 (when George W. Bush leaves office), America will have had 22 years of divided government. For only 10 of those years were the White House and both houses of Congress controlled by the same party. (For 7 of the remaining years the president had a majority in one House but not the other.) Expect the new Congress to take its monitoring role more seriously.

One way in which President Bush will feel this most keenly will be in his ability to shape the federal courts. 'Bush's power to Shape Courts Ended by Election Loss' was a headline to a James Rowley article on www.bloomberg.com. He quoted a former Senate Republican aide Manuel Miranda as saying that 'the Bush presidency is over with regard to judges'. With a Republican-controlled Senate, George W. Bush was able to elevate John Roberts and Samuel Alito to the Supreme Court and appointed over a quarter (46 out of 179) of the nation's appeal court judges.

Another way in which President Bush might notice the change of climate on Capitol Hill is in trade agreements. Democrat Max Baucus of Montana, the new chairman of the Senate Finance Committee, made an early indication that he would not support a renewal of the President's so-called 'fast-track trade authority' – the administration's power to call for simple up-or-down votes in Congress on trade agreements without having them subject to amendment.

But before one writes off President Bush as a lame duck it is worth remembering three things. First, the President didn't get either of his major pieces of legislation — social security reform and immigration reform — through the Republican-controlled Congress in 2006. So what's new if Congress obstructs the President? Second, George W. Bush is now free from electoral considerations. He might be tempted to make more bold compromises to achieve what he wants on Capitol Hill. Finally, the Democrats will need to have something to show in 2008 for their 2-year control of Congress. Blaming non-candidate Bush is unlikely to go down well with the voters in 2 years' time. So Bush and Pelosi might just settle for a marriage of convenience. Stranger things have happened.

Who's who in American politics 2007

Executive branch

President — George W. Bush
Vice-President — Dick Cheney

The cabinet

Secretary of State — Condoleezza Rice
Secretary of Defense — Robert Gates
Secretary of the Treasury — Henry Paulson
Secretary of Agriculture — Michael Johanns
Secretary of the Interior — Dick Kempthorne
Attorney General (Justice Department) — Alberto Gonzales
Secretary of Commerce — Carlos Gutierrez
Secretary of Labor — Elaine Chao
Secretary of Health and Human Services — Michael Leavitt
Secretary of Education — Margaret Spellings
Secretary of Housing and Urban Development — Alphonso Jackson
Secretary of Transportation — Mary Peters
Secretary of Energy — Samuel Bodman
Secretary of Veterans' Affairs — Jim Nicholson
Secretary of Homeland Security — Michael Chertoff

Executive Office of the President personnel

White House Chief of Staff — Joshua Bolten
Director of Office of Management and Budget — Rob Portman
National Security Adviser — Stephen Hadley
Chairman of Council of Economic Advisers — Gregory Mankiw
Assistant to the President for Legislative Affairs — Candida Perotti Wolff
Trade Representative — Susan Schwab
Administrator of Environmental Protection Agency — Stephen Johnson
Press Secretary — Tony Snow

Other executive branch personnel

Director of Central Intelligence Agency (CIA) — General Michael Hayden
Director of Federal Bureau of Investigation (FBI) — Robert Mueller
Chairman of the Joint Chiefs of Staff (JCS) — General Peter Pace

Legislative branch

President *Pro Tempore* of the Senate	Robert Byrd (D — West Virginia)
Senate Majority Leader	Harry Reid (D — Nevada)
Senate Majority Whip	Richard Durbin (D — Illinois)
Senate Minority Leader	Mitch McConnell (R — Kentucky)
Senate Minority Whip	Trent Lott (R — Mississippi)
Speaker of the House of Representatives	Nancy Pelosi (D — California)
House Majority Leader	Steny Hoyer (D — Maryland)
House Minority Leader	John Boehner (R — Ohio)
House Majority Whip	James Clyburn (D — South Carolina)
House Minority Whip	Roy Blunt (R — Missouri)

Senate Standing Committee chairs

Agriculture, Nutrition and Forestry	Tom Harkin	Iowa
Appropriations	Robert Byrd	West Virginia
Armed Services	Carl Levin	Michigan
Banking, Housing and Urban Affairs	Christopher Dodd	Connecticut
Budget	Kent Conrad	North Dakota
Commerce, Science and Transportation	Daniel Inouye	Hawaii
Energy and Natural Resources	Jeff Bingaman	New Mexico
Environment and Public Works	Barbara Boxer	California
Finance	Max Baucus	Montana
Foreign Relations	Joseph Biden	Maryland
Health, Education, Labor and Pensions	Edward Kennedy	Massachusetts
Homeland Security and Governmental Affairs	Joseph Lieberman	Connecticut
Judiciary	Patrick Leahy	Vermont
Rules and Administration	Dianne Feinstein	California
Small Business and Entrepreneurship	John Kerry	Massachusetts
Veterans' Affairs	Daniel Akaka	Hawaii

House Standing Committee chairs

Agriculture	Collin Peterson	Minnesota
Appropriations	David Obey	Wisconsin
Armed Services	Ike Skelton	Missouri
Budget	John Spratt	South Carolina
Education and the Workforce	George Miller	California
Energy and Commerce	John Dingell	Michigan
Financial Services	Barney Frank	Massachusetts
Government Reform	Henry Waxman	California
Homeland Security	Bennie Thompson	Mississippi

International Relations	Tom Lantos	California
Judiciary	John Conyers	Michigan
Resources	Nick Rahall	West Virginia
Rules	Louise Slaughter	New York
Science	Bart Gordon	Tennessee
Small Business	Nydia Velázquez	New York
Transportation and Infrastructure	James Oberstar	Minnesota
Veterans' Affairs	Bob Filner	California
Ways and Means	Charles Rangell	New York

Judicial branch

		President who appointed	Year appointed
Chief Justice	John Roberts	George W. Bush	2005
Associate Justices	John Paul Stevens	Ford	1975
	Antonin Scalia	Reagan	1986
	Anthony Kennedy	Reagan	1987
	David Souter	Bush	1990
	Clarence Thomas	Bush	1991
	Ruth Bader Ginsburg	Clinton	1993
	Stephen Breyer	Clinton	1994
	Samuel Alito	George W. Bush	2006